READING AND REMEDIAL READING

Reading and remedial reading

A. E. TANSLEY

ROUTLEDGE AND KEGAN PAUL, LONDON

First published 1967
by Routledge *&* Kegan Paul *Limited*
Broadway House, 68–74 *Carter Lane*
London, EC4V 5EL

Reprinted (twice) 1969, 1972, 1973 *&* 1974

Printed in Great Britain by
Unwin Brothers Limited
The Gresham Press, Old Woking, Surrey, England
A member of the Staples Printing Group

ISBN 0 7100 2169 0 (c)

ISBN 0 7100 7468 9 (p)

Contents

Appendices

FIGURES

Preface

This book is based on a number of articles describing the normal reading programme in the author's school and the diagnosis and treatment of acute difficulties in learning to read. They were originally written for the benefit of the school staff who found them so informative and useful that it was decided to publish them in order to make them available to a wider public—staffs and students of University Education Departments and Colleges of Education, educational psychologists, remedial teachers, special-school teachers, primary-school teachers, advanced students taking specialist courses in remedial education or in the education of handicapped pupils, and medical officers in the School Health Service.

Although the work described was confined mainly to an atypical population of so-called educationally subnormal/maladjusted children (many of whom showed signs of possible damage to the central nervous system), I believe that the methods and techniques given are applicable to all children, irrespective of levels of intelligence, who are experiencing difficulty in learning to read. Some of the claims made must obviously be speculative, since they are based on results obtained from a small population. Some of them are also based only on empirical evidence. The results we have achieved are most encouraging, however, and have been tested by countless expert visitors from this country and abroad. I hope, therefore, that our methods and suggestions will be followed by many other workers—the results they get will be a sure guide as to whether our claims are justified.

I would like to express my sincere gratitude to all my colleagues at St. Francis Residential School, Birmingham, for their wonderful support. My particular thanks are due to Mrs. I. Squires, Mr. G. B. Adams, Mrs. C. Perry and Dr. R. J. Stanley.

A. E. TANSLEY

Birmingham, 1966

PART ONE

The teaching of reading

1 Some general considerations

There have undoubtedly been improvements in the reading attainments of children during the past ten years and these have been reflected in the higher attainments of school leavers.[1] Although reliable figures are not available, it is reasonably certain that fewer children are leaving school illiterate or semi-literate. These improvements have been due to a determined effort on the part of the L.E.A.'s and teachers to tackle the problem of backwardness. The provision of more special schools, special classes, remedial departments and diagnostic clinics; the provision of more courses and lectures for teachers; and an expansion (although limited and inadequate) in research into the reading process and teaching materials, have all played a part in raising reading standards.

Nevertheless, there is no room for complacency. Still too many children have reading attainments which are inadequate or too far below average. Too many children are allowed to experience difficulties which could be avoided. Even were this not the case, there is reason to believe that the present norms for reading tests could be raised with better teaching, more appropriate methods and improved teaching materials. If improvements are to be made, it is essential that some of the accepted traditions and standards should be questioned and

[1] *Progress in Reading*, Educ. Pamph., No. 50, H.M.S.O., 1966.

tested. The following are some of the questions which teachers should be asking themselves:

1 Are the present programmes for fostering reading readiness sufficiently scientific?

2 To what extent can training in language skills and perceptual abilities hasten readiness?

3 How many children might reasonably be expected to be reading fluently before they begin formal schooling?

4 Is there a 'best' method for the majority of children? If so, what is it?

5 Which generally comes first—visual or auditory readiness?

6 What perceptual abilities are involved in mechanical reading?

7 Can the development of these abilities be hastened by training?

8 What skills and abilities are involved in phonic analysis and synthesis? Can these be trained?

9 Can reading speed be increased by the use of suitable visual aids?

10 Can backwardness in reading be reduced by the early diagnosis of visuo-spatial and auditory difficulties and by timely remedial measures?

11 What are the advantages and/or disadvantages of new alphabets in achieving *lasting* improvements in reading attainments, and as remedial techniques?

12 What methods are most likely to lead to improved comprehension of what is read?

13 What contributions do oral and written work make to the general improvement of reading and language development?

Reliable answers to many of these questions will not be available until much more controlled research has been done. Some answers may never become available because when comparisons of different methods are undertaken too many uncontrollable variables, such as teaching ability, cultural background, levels of motivation, are bound to be present.

Nevertheless, those teachers who have been concerned with devising methods and writing materials to improve reading levels generally and to overcome backwardness in particular are able to suggest how better attainments might be achieved. The suggestions arise from a mixture of research, experiment and empiricism. At this point, it is perhaps appropriate to stress the significant discovery that methods and techniques which have proved successful with backward readers are equally successful with bright children. A reading scheme which has been 'programmed' to ensure success for E.S.N. children has been highly successful with more intelligent children. The learning processes are the same; the difference is a matter of speed of learning which depends upon the ability to make abstractions and generalizations, levels of aspiration, and degrees of motivation.

This book describes methods and techniques which have proved successful with backward children. It will also deal with certain new developments in diagnosis and treatment of cases of extreme reading difficulty.

The following are some of the principles upon which a well-balanced reading scheme should be based.

1 A comprehensive programme of reading readiness activities and training is essential.

2 Sensory and perceptual difficulties should be diagnosed and treated as early as possible.

3 Visual readiness normally precedes auditory readiness.

4 Due regard must be paid to individual differences.

5 Systematic teaching yields better results than incidental teaching.

6 Reading must be viewed as one element in an integrated programme for language development, i.e. it must be allied to oral work, controlled and free written work, spelling and dramatic activities.

7 In the early stages a basic sight vocabulary should be used. This vocabulary should be selected on the basis of word frequency in the spoken and reading language of young children.

8 In motivation, interest is important, but cumulative feelings of success are absolutely essential. Books should therefore be sufficiently well-graded to ensure continuing success through attention to learning load increments, repetition and consolidation.

9 All children can be taught to read unless the I.Q. is less than 50–55 and unless there is acute pathology of the sensory organs or central nervous system or mental ill-health.

10 Teaching of reading should ensure that mechanical reading and comprehension develop commensurately.

11 Controlled supplementary reading is essential until a reading age of about 9 years has been achieved.

2 Reading readiness

Experience with severely backward children, particularly older children, reveals that one of the principal causes of failure is teaching which has failed to take into account the importance of not introducing children to learning situations before they are ready. This is particularly true in the teaching of reading, largely because reading assumes greater importance in a highly literate culture and is thus taught as soon as possible. Teachers are generally anxious, indeed over-anxious, to 'get on with reading'. It is this anxiety which often leads to children being pushed into reading before they are ready. It is important, therefore, that all teachers concerned with young and backward children should be fully conversant with the educational and psychological principles involved in reading readiness. They should be trained in the recognition of readiness signs. They should be capable of organizing activities and providing experiences which will foster readiness and possibly hasten it.

In devising a reading readiness programme, it is important to remember that intellectual, physical, emotional and social developments are involved. It is also important to realize that growth in these four areas of development may be uneven. A child may be physically and intellectually ready but be too immature emotionally and socially to be able to benefit from teaching. Yet another may be emotionally stable and well-adapted socially but be intellectually retarded or be suffering from some physical or sensory handicap. Nevertheless, it often happens that a child can make a satisfactory beginning to reading even when readiness in one or more of the areas of development has not been reached. An example of this would be the maladjusted child whose maladjustment arose from reading failure. The 'cure' in such a case centres round remedial education to achieve feelings of success in reading, since overcoming the reading difficulty will remove the cause of emotional disturbance. Two further aspects of readiness must be stressed. One is that readiness is itself a developing, dynamic process. The learner is always getting ready for the next step in the learning process. This is why the 'programming' of learning situations is so vital. The second is that all learning is a means of helping the individual to accept, analyse, integrate and appropriately respond to a variety of stimuli which impinge upon him in a variety of sensory modes: seeing, hearing, touching, smelling, tasting. The efficiency with which this process is performed can only be assessed by what the child says or does, i.e. vocally or by motor activity. The readiness programme must therefore be based on a multi-sensory approach and must involve the child totally. Thus the child must learn to listen as well as to speak, to observe as well as to draw, describe or imitate, and to respond in mime as well as in words.

It is not the intention of this book to give a comprehensive description of all the forms of play, types of activities and experiences which should be included in a reading readiness programme. This can be found in many textbooks dealing with the subject. However, the following may be useful in helping teachers and parents to assess readiness.

1 Readiness in language development

1 Is the child interested in listening to stories?

2 Can he relate the main ideas of a story in correct sequence?

3 Is he interested in and can he talk about pictures?

4 Can he describe a picture in some detail, e.g. can he say what is happening or what is likely to happen?

5 Can he talk about what he has seen, done or heard?

6 Is he interested in trying to read signs or advertisements?

7 Does he use good sentences in his normal conversation?

8 Does he know the common nursery rhymes and does he like to make play with words and sounds?

2 Readiness in physical and sensory development

1 Does his eyesight appear to be normal?

2 Does he hear within normal limits?

3 Does he listen to commands and carry them out efficiently?

4 Is he active, curious and in good health?

5 Does he use his body with good co-ordination?

6 Does he appear to have a good sense of rhythm?

7 Does he know the primary colours?

8 Does he use a pencil, crayons or paint brush with reasonable efficiency?

9 Can he draw a recognizable picture of a human figure and a house?

10 Can he draw a reasonably straight line of about 6 in. in length?

11 Can he do simple jigsaws?

12 Is his speech clearly articulated?

3 Readiness in emotional and social development

1 Does he play well with other children?

2 Does he share his belongings with others?

3 Is he not easily upset?

4 Is he not easily distracted from what he is doing?

5 Does he accept changes in routine without undue stress?

The answers to these questions will give some indication about the child's degree of readiness. The questions themselves suggest activities which may be organized to foster the development of readiness. The following chapter will deal with a new perceptual training programme which could be used to supplement the more general approach suggested above. It must be stressed, however, that good language development based on wide experiences, rich opportunities for conversation, listening and discussing, and spontaneous and structured play is an essential part of a reading readiness scheme.

3 Training perceptual abilities[1]

Perceptual abilities and reading

Research has not yet demonstrated unequivocally what perceptual abilities are important in reading. However, we can postulate with some degree of certainty those abilities which appear to be involved. These are: hand–eye co-ordination, visual copying, visual memory, pattern and figure closure, visual rhythm, visual sequencing, auditory rhythm and sequencing, visual discrimination and form appreciation. The relative importance of these has not been reliably established but research and experience tend to demonstrate the following:

* 1 Success in the visual aspects of reading depends upon the ability to perceive quickly, to hold a 'gestalt' in mind and to close a 'gestalt'. The ability to keep a 'whole' in mind should not be affected by visual distractions. Thus, efficient reading involves the ability to keep a whole word or phrase in mind while simultaneously attention is paid to parts of the word or phrase. Without this ability there is a failure in discrimination and particular confusion over words which are of similar visual pattern.

[1] The ideas and methods described in this and the following chapter will be incorporated in *Early to Read* to be published later this year by E. J. Arnold & Son, Butterley Street, Leeds 10.

2 Success in the auditory aspects depends upon the ability to discriminate between sounds, to remember sounds and repeat them rhythmically in sequence. A good auditory memory and rhythmic sense are essential.

Russian research has demonstrated the importance of language as a regulator of activity and behaviour. Experimental work has shown that language is also involved in perceptual activity and should be used in the training of perceptual abilities. In St. Francis School we have demonstrated that dramatic improvements in the perceptual abilities of brain-damaged children can be made by systematic perceptual training coupled with language training. The language used in training has to include those words and parts of speech which assist the child in structuring his visual perceptions. Conversation during training should therefore concentrate on adjectives, comparatives and superlatives, prepositions, adverbs and adverbial phrases. However, specific training of words should be avoided since this does not lead to generalization of meanings. For example, if a child is taught the word 'circle' as applying to a particular circle he has drawn or to a particular object, his perception of circularity will be meaningless unless he can generalize from the specific training to apply it to all circles or objects with circularity inherent in them, e.g. plates, cups, saucers, light switches, telephone dials, etc.

A perceptual training programme

1 *Training in form perception*

Pre-school children and older backward or perceptually handicapped children need and benefit from training in form perception. Normally, such training is provided by surrounding the child with toys and objects which give wide experiences in handling and fitting together, and by tracing and drawing. A graded series of jigsaw puzzles is also helpful, particularly if the child is encouraged to talk about what he is doing.

Some children, however, may require more specific training in the recognition and drawing of shapes and forms. For example, give the child a big collection of circles, squares, oblongs and triangles of various sizes and colours. Ask him to put them in families and to suggest names for them, and finally teach the actual geometric names. Now use the shapes as templates and teach the child to draw round them. When he can do this ask him to fill in the shapes with colour. Encourage him to discover how shapes may be combined to make new shapes, e.g. a square and a triangle to make a house, two similar squares to make an oblong, etc.

The training might then be advanced to considering differences in size—big circles, little circles, middle circles, and so on. The child may be taught to seriate and to classify forms according to shape and size, and a third variable of colour may be introduced. Exercises like the following are of great educational value.

1 Put all the triangles together.

2 Now sort them into big triangles and little triangles.

3 Look at the little triangles—can we sort them again? (Colour introduced here.)

4 What things can you see in this picture or in the room which are like triangles? squares? circles?

When the child is capable of recognizing two-dimensional form, solids may be introduced in a similar way.

The child should now be shown how he might be able to communicate by using the shapes. Make pictures of, say, a house, a boat, a bird, etc., by using the four shapes. Show the child each picture in turn, give the shapes required, and ask him to 'make' the picture. We say to our children, 'Suppose you could not talk; use these shapes to tell me there is a bird outside.' This type of exercise helps to show the child that shapes and their uses are important, and to indicate the role of pictures and, later, writing in communication.

Our training in form perception includes intensive work on improving the child's body image. We start by using pictures of human beings stuck on manilla card and cut across the middle. The child puts the two parts together and learns the meaning of top half and bottom half. Next we cut the card horizontally into three equal pieces—the child now learns top, middle and bottom. Succeeding cards are cut into increasing numbers of parts, using horizontal, vertical and oblique cuts. Finally the picture is presented in the more usual jigsaw form. This work, combined with the learning of body parts, putting together sectioned dolls, and making bodies out of plasticine produces great improvements in the child's awareness of his own body, in his ability to draw a human figure and in skill with jigsaw puzzles.

Play materials which will enrich and expand this training in form perception are readily available and should be used at the appropriate time. Free play with paint, plasticine, clay, mosaics, wet sand and variously shaped blocks should be encouraged all the time. It is also important to give haptic training in which the child is not allowed to see the various forms and shapes but has to identify or classify by touch and movement. Here again the child should be encouraged to talk about what he is doing, e.g. this is a round shape, this has sharp corners, one side is longer than the other, this has three sides, this is long and narrow, etc.

It is perhaps worthy of mention at this juncture that children known to be brain-damaged have responded extremely well to this training. For example, Royston, who had an occipital lobectomy when he was nine, has made wonderful progress. Two years ago his Binet I.Q. was given as 44 and he was unable to control his hand movements. When he started a movement he was unable to stop voluntarily; he could not draw a line or a circle; he was extremely restless and distractible. Now he can write his name and other words, can draw a circle, triangle and oblong, and has a sight vocabulary of 170–180 words, and at his level, reads quite fluently with understanding. It is of course impossible to determine what part of his progress may be attributed to perceptual training. However, it would seem that it has helped him considerably.

Loraine was unable to do very simple jigsaws; twelve months later she was very adept indeed at completing 50-

piece puzzles with understanding instead of by trial-and-error. She was unable to read but has now completed our 16 pre-phonic readers, made an encouraging start with phonics, and has reached a mechanical reading age of 9 years.

2 *Training in hand–eye motor co-ordination*

Control of eye movements and co-ordination of hand and eye are obvious prerequisites of efficient reading and writing.

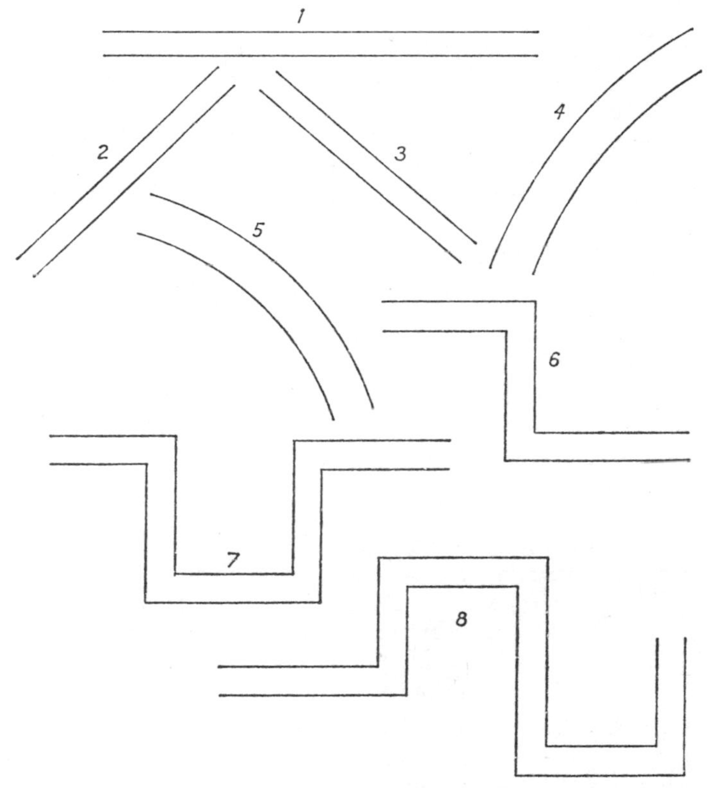

Figure 1 Hand-eye co-ordination

Most children develop these without actual training, by incidental learning through sensori-motor operations involved in play and natural body activity. However, some children need training, and perhaps all children would develop co-ordination more quickly if they received help. Games and toys which encourage hand–eye co-ordination should be used, e.g. running cars along imaginary roads and trains along tracks; moving animals between fences; moving counters in games such as Ludo and Snakes and Ladders, etc.

Specific training we have used involves encouraging the child to draw continuous lines between given spaces (Fig. 1) or joining dots in a set order. The spaces vary from ½ in. wide to ⅛ in. wide and drawing continuous lines in them gives practice in moving from left to right, up and down, through upward and downward curves, and through right angles. In joining dots many changes of direction are made and particular practice is provided in crossing the body mid-line in both directions.

For perceptually handicapped children the above exercises are preceded by organized play activities and by exercises involving less-refined movements, using blackboards and chalk. With such children, the use of speech has been found to be very helpful in inhibiting unnecessary movement. Thus, we have taught them to say, 'Steady, steady, down, down, stop; turn, across, across, stop; turn, up, up, stop!' Eventually with increasing control over irradiated movement the speech is inner-vocalized and presumably becomes truly internalized in the end when good co-ordination has been achieved. We have made use of suggestions given by Luria,[1] and our experience certainly endorses his general thesis.

Exercises such as those described provide practice in hand–eye movements and help to develop within the child a sense of direction from side to side and up and down. Combined with training in the discrimination of reversed drawings and models, they also appear to overcome the reversal difficulties

[1] A. R. Luria, *The Role of Speech in the Regulation of Normal and Abnormal Behaviour* (Pergamon Press: Oxford 1961).

which are often associated with backwardness, e.g. 'no' for 'on', 'saw' for 'was'.

Mirror writing is also likely to be avoided.

3 *Training in visual copying*

For this, we first use a graded series of matchstick figures for the child to copy. The figures are stuck on stiff card and the child has to copy them by using spent matches. When the child fails to reproduce a figure correctly, training is given.

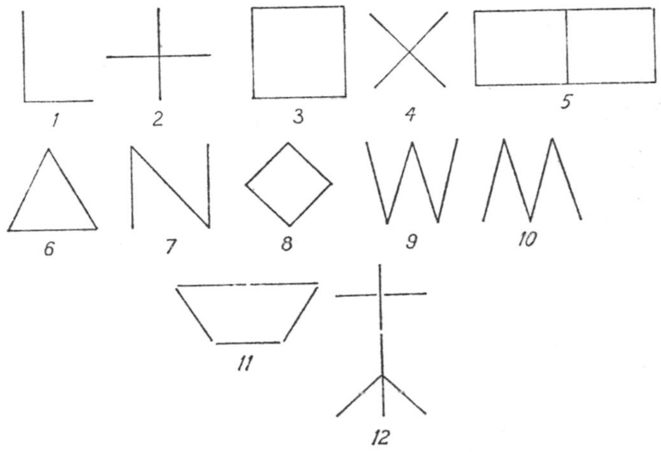

Figure 2 Visual copying

The child traces over the figure with finger contact; he is helped to analyse it by considering size, direction of matches, contiguity of matches, whether the figure is 'closed' or 'open'.

The copying of matchstick figures is accompanied by the copying of figures and patterns drawn by the teacher either on a blackboard or on stiff card. We have now established what appears to be a correct order of difficulty for these figures and patterns. Some are given in *Figure 2* but teachers will enjoy experimenting with their own material, and incidentally learn a good deal in the process.

Extensions of this training in copying will, of course, be included in Art and Craft, in the beginning-of-writing patterns, in copying mosaics, and in jigsaws.

4 *Training in visual memory*

The figures and patterns used in *3* should now be used for training visual recall and retention. The figure to be remembered is displayed for about five seconds and then the child is asked to reproduce it from memory. When difficulty arises specific training accompanied by language is given. Research and experience show that giving each figure a name helps recall.

5 *Training in completion and closure*

The ability to 'close' a figure in the absence of part of it appears to be significant in reading and perceptual activity generally. We therefore present the child with incomplete figures and patterns for him to 'close'. The incomplete figures and patterns are presented on individual cards and the child[1] either points to the missing part(s) or, using tracing paper, traces over the figure and completes it. We also use specially prepared drawings in which only part of an object or action is visible and ask the child to describe what the object is or what is happening.

This training in 'closure' and visual imagery is particularly valuable both for developing perceptual ability and for encouraging language and concept development.

6 *Training in appreciation of visual rhythm*

For this, we use a graded series of repeating visual patterns. The child has to discover the pattern and continue it across the page of an exercise book or prepared strips of paper. The child is encouraged to talk about the pattern (e.g. cross, cross, circle; down line, across line, etc.), and thereby learns to make

[1] We now use talc or acetate sheets and chinagraph, or similar, pencils.

an association between auditory and visual sequences. Pre-writing patterns are also used as an extension of this training.

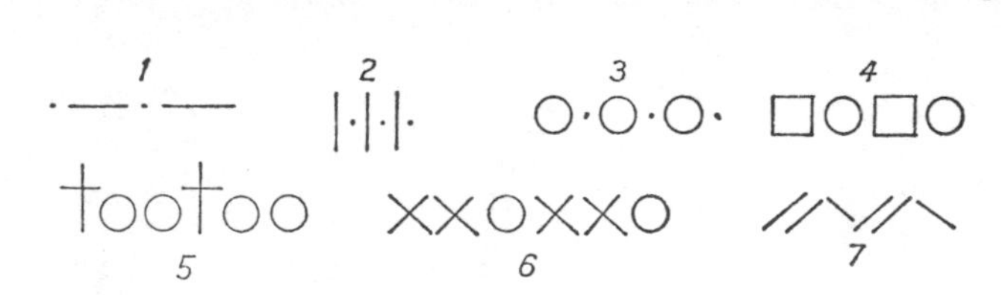

Figure 3 Visual rhythms: samples

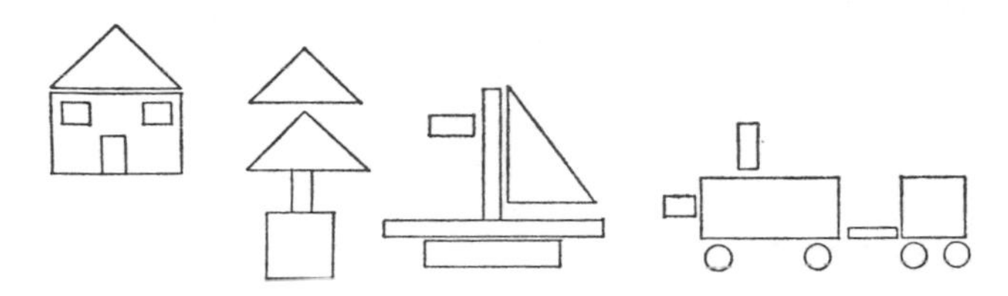

Figure 4 Using shapes: samples

7 *Training in visual sequencing*

An ability to remember visual sequences is obviously involved in the mechanical reading process, and particularly in the more difficult process of spelling. In both processes, of course, there is close association, particularly in phonically regular words, between visual and auditory sequencing. Exploratory work we have done using the Kirk and McCarthy Illinois Test of Psycholinguistic Abilities (see Chapter 10, p. 115) appears to demonstrate that the vast majority of backward children are particularly deficient in sequencing abilities. Training in these abilities is therefore particularly important.

For training in visual sequencing, we use individual cards with pictures of well-known objects and geometric figures. For instance, we show the child card pictures of a chimney and a window. These are placed side by side, the child looks at them for about five seconds and after the cards have been scattered, he is asked to place them side by side in the correct

Teacher's card

	VISUAL SEQUENCING show 5 secs.
1	Chimney Window
2	Window Apple
3	Chimney Tree
4	Apple Tree Window
5	○ □
6	□ △ ○
7	□ ○ ◠
8	⌂ ○ △ ○
9	◠ △ □ □
10	○ △ △ ◠
11	△ ⌂ □ ○
12	○ □ ⌂ △ ◠

Figure 5 Visual sequencing

order as previously demonstrated. We then introduce a picture of an apple. The window and apple cards are now placed side by side and displayed for five seconds. The *three* picture cards are now scattered and the child is asked to repeat the demonstrated exercise: a fourth card of a tree is then introduced and the sequences are increased to three and four cards.

The picture cards are then collected and sequences using geometric figures are used similarly. We use a square, rectangle, triangle, circle, trapezium and semi-circle and we train the child to remember five or six figures in sequence. As in previous exercises we make much use of language and the children are encouraged to give names to the figures. Some children can perform the tasks purely visually, but the majority need speech to achieve quick success.

The same progression of sequences may be used for training auditory memory. The individual sequences are displayed for five seconds each; the sequence is removed and the child *names* it.

8 Training in temporal sequencing

This aspect of the perceptual training programme is to encourage the child to place pictures, diagrams and patterns in temporal order. The child is shown, say, five pictures of a house in various stages of erection. He is asked to arrange them in time order and relate the story they tell. Much valuable language work is involved in this type of activity, e.g. the meaning of such words as *first*, *second*, *third*, *fourth*, *last*, *later*, *next*, *earlier*, *before*, *after* and *middle*, as well as words to describe individual pictures, can be taught with emphasis on understanding and usage.

Other sequences we use include a flower at different stages of growth; a car being assembled; getting up; going to bed; growing up; a letter being written and posted; a cake being made. The number of individual cards in the sequences increases from four to ten. The picture sequences may be followed first by cards of diagrams and patterns in various stages of completion and then by more complicated picture sequences similar to those used in non-verbal tests of intelligence, e.g. Wechsler Intelligence Scale for Children—Performance Sub-Test for Picture Arrangement.

9 *Training in visual discrimination*

The training exercises we use here are usually found in non-verbal group tests of intelligence and in books designed to hasten or test reading readiness. It is very likely that the ability involved in discriminating between almost identical pictures is trainable, particularly when language and a multi-sensory approach are used. The children we have trained have shown remarkable improvements in appreciating sameness and difference in pictures and designs even at very refined levels of distinction.

We again use series of cards 'programmed' in order of difficulty. The cards are in sets of five or six with two cards in each set identical. The child is shown one of the identical cards and has to search through the remaining cards to find the one which is 'exactly the same' as the one given to him. In every case, he has to explain the reasons for his choice and for his rejection of all the other cards in the set. The differences in the cards involve omissions, rotations, lateral inversions, size variation, and colour differences. Other variations of this type of exercise could well be used, e.g. find which is the 'odd man out'; which is correct or which is silly; which is the missing piece or feature.

Training in this type of exercise is also extremely useful in avoiding reversal difficulties, particularly if it is given at the time when the child is in the process of structuring his ideas of laterality and directionality (generally at four to five years of age for the majority of children). It also, of course, provides excellent opportunities for language development and for developing ideas of likeness and difference which are so vital in concept formation and growth in the ability to classify, two fundamental aspects of intellectual development and the acquisition of learning.

10 *Training in auditory sequencing and rhythm*

Thus far, the suggested perceptual training programme has concentrated primarily on the visuo-spatial and visuo-motor aspects of perception. Reading, of course, also involves auditory perception and discrimination, and a fully comprehensive programme must include training in auditory skills. Those teachers who work with backward children will appreciate the difficulties many children appear to experience in auditory discrimination and auditory recall. These difficulties become all the more apparent when attempts are made to teach phonic analysis and blending. Frequently children are able to learn the sounds of letters and phonograms, but are unable to remember them in sequence in a word and to blend them rhythmically. Our work with very retarded children has revealed that the majority of those who have particular difficulty in reading, and especially the phonic aspects of it, are lacking in rhythmicity and have poor auditory memory.

Leslie is a typical example. He had been admitted to the school at thirteen years of age when he was totally illiterate and greatly lacking in self-confidence. We had no organized perceptual training at the time but he responded reasonably well to our reading readiness scheme and began to acquire a sight vocabulary. He took two years to learn 200 words and his reading age rose gradually to a 6½-year level. This is the level at which most of our children begin a systematic programme of phonic training. Leslie failed to respond to this programme and he became quite depressed about his lack of progress. He had a slight hearing loss but this was not sufficient to account for his failure. It was decided, therefore, to give him extra individual remedial work in phonic drills, but this also failed to produce any success. More or less by chance, I thought about testing his ability to repeat simple rhythms tapped out to him. He was unable to repeat three equally spaced taps. It appeared likely that this inability was probably associated with his difficulty, especially when many more children with similar difficulties were tested and found to have the same disability.

It was this experience which made us realize the importance of training children in auditory sequencing and rhythm. The following exercises and activities are used in the training programme.

1 Repeating short sentences perfectly.

2 Learning and saying jingles and rhymes.

3 Listening to and obeying commands.

4 Marching and dancing to simple rhythms.

5 Scribbling or finger painting in time to rhythms.

6 Singing rhythmical songs and action songs.

7 Following a sequence of directions.

8 Sound blending.

9 Telling sequences of events in a story either read or presented in pictures.

10 Drawing a series of figures or patterns after they have been presented visually.

11 Selecting from a series of pictures or geometric figures the two, three or four named.

In addition to those, however, we have concentrated particularly on trying to develop a sense of rhythm. This is done by using the following techniques:

1 We use Morse Code symbols and ask the child to repeat the rhythm of a given letter using 'dah' for dashes and 'di' for dots. Thus the teacher says 'Dah, dah' and the child repeats after her. With young children we use the following rhythms:

—— ——, · ·, —— ·, · ——, —— —— ——, · · ·,
—— —— ·, · · ——, —— · ——, —— —— · ·,
· · —— ——, —— · —— ·, —— · —— · ——

More complicated rhythms may, of course, be used.

2 The same rhythms are now presented by tapping out either by hand on a table or by striking one stick against another. The children repeat the rhythms as presented. This is more

difficult than saying the rhythms. We therefore encourage the children to use sounds to accompany the tapping.

3 We now teach the child to associate the auditory rhythm with a visual pattern. Thus, for two long taps the child writes —— —— and for long, short, long, writes —— · ——. After the child has written the rhythm he repeats it by tapping.

4 Further training is given by using percussion instruments to develop the ability to remember sequences and rhythms. The following is a selection of the exercises used.

   a Counting and reproducing a given number of taps either demonstrated or requested by the teacher.
   b Copying and continuing a rhythm initiated by the teacher using variation in accent.
   c Tapping out individual words or well-known tunes and nursery rhymes with and without speech.
   d Tapping rhythms with the unpreferred hand.
   e Tapping rhythms with both hands simultaneously.
   f Tapping rhythms while moving.
   g Tapping rhythms to music or while singing.

Many young children and older backward children have great difficulty in coping with these exercises. However, patient training can achieve marked progress particularly if the performing of the exercises is reinforced by speech and movement, and by teaching the child to watch as well as listen to the rhythm.

Some children are so deficient in rhythmicity that individual training is necessary. With these, the teacher has to move parts of the child's body (fingers, hands, legs, head, trunk) in time with the given rhythm, and gradually, over a period of time, give less and less physical assistance. The child should also feel rhythms, e.g. by placing fingertips lightly on a drum or tambourine as the teacher beats a rhythm. Beating out rhythms on parts of the child's body is also helpful, the child being asked to tap out the rhythm or continue it with the teacher.

Our experience suggests that lack of rhythmicity is closely correlated with reading deficiency and with brain damage. Nevertheless, there is reason to believe that provided training as described above is given sufficiently early, significant improvements may result.

4 The beginning of reading

Some general considerations

Although the perceptual training programme has been given in full in the previous chapter, it is not necessary for the child to have completed the whole programme before a start may be made in the beginnings of reading *per se*. The results of our training tend to indicate, however, that a child unable to do most of the exercises in form appreciation, visual copying and visual discrimination is not likely to make progress in acquiring a basic stock of sight words. Children who do make progress are still given perceptual training until they can complete the programme satisfactorily. It is absolutely essential to continue training in auditory sequencing and rhythm for children who need it, in order to avoid difficulties later on when the child needs the assistance of phonic analysis and synthesis in developing quick and accurate word recognition. In other words, it is essential to develop phonic readiness if continuing success in reading is to be achieved.

When the child displays a readiness to start reading, the problem of which method and materials should be used has to be solved. It is, of course, undesirable to teach *all* children by a rigidly uniform method, and a dogmatic ruling about books and materials would be unacceptable to teachers. It is a cardinal principle in British education that the teacher must be free to decide on these matters. Nevertheless, wise decisions can only be taken by teachers who have been well trained by experts who are up-to-date in their education theory and practice and who can demonstrate good results.

The following is a description of a reading method which for some ten years has been producing consistently good results in the author's school. No other claim is made for it, although there is plenty of evidence that it has been extremely well received elsewhere. The method is based on the following premises, some of which have been mentioned earlier.

1 Reading is a developmental process and a reading programme should be so organized as to assist the development. The programme has therefore to be based on a sound knowledge of the developmental psychology involved in learning to associate visual and auditory patterns, to extract meaning from these, and to interpret and apply these meanings for the growth of knowledge and enrichment of ideas.

2 The rate of development is dependent upon individual differences. Teachers must therefore be capable of recognizing these differences and able to organize the reading programme and materials to meet individual reading needs.

3 A good reading programme consists of four parts: the development of readiness; the acquisition of a sight vocabulary of words which occur frequently in children's reading and spoken vocabulary; the development of independent reading by the use of phonic analysis and synthesis and other word recognition techniques; the development of speedy, relaxed silent reading for content, ideas and pleasure.

4 Generally, children achieve visual readiness for reading before auditory readiness.

5 Reading is viewed as an integral part of a language programme. As such it must be taught in relation to other

forms of communication: speaking, listening and writing. An over-emphasis on mechanical reading to the detriment of comprehension, oral and written expression, and opportunities for listening should be avoided.

6 Developmental reading can only be achieved by systematic teaching. Particularly in the early stages, uniformity of method is essential for the majority of children. Teachers who deal with older backward readers are familiar with the child who appears to have been taught by almost as many methods as the number of teachers who have taught him. He is, therefore, thoroughly confused and often has acute feelings of frustration and hopelessness. It is thus very important that the staff of a school should get together to arrive at a reading method acceptable to all, thus ensuring continuity throughout the early classes in the school. This does not necessarily mean that schools must adopt one particular reading scheme. It does mean that schemes adopted should be based on identical methods, similar vocabulary loads, and appropriate grading.

7 Reading difficulties should be discovered as early as possible and appropriate remedial measures taken.

8 Children learn to read by reading. The reading programme must therefore use a wide range of interesting, well-graded and well-organized supplementary reading.

9 The ideas and concepts acquired from reading should be enriched by discussion, study of word meanings, dramatic activities, art and craft, and direct and indirect experiences such as visits, films, filmstrips, slides and recordings.

Acquiring a sight vocabulary

If it is agreed that learning to read should start by the teaching of a sight vocabulary, it is necessary to decide what the content and size of this vocabulary should be. The words selected have to be useful, interesting, learnable and comprehensible and, if our thesis is correct, there should be sufficient of them to lead into readiness for the use of phonic and other clues in later word recognition. Research into the early spoken vocabulary of children and the words used in first reading books has resulted in several lists of words to be used in selecting a basic sight vocabulary. A study of the work of Thorndike,[1] Dale, Dolch,[3] Tansley and Gulliford,[4] McNally and Murray, Burroughs[6] and Gates[7] will give a very reasonable guide to which words ought to be included. It is suggested that before teachers choose primers and supplementary readers for young children some of these lists should be consulted. They should, however, keep in mind the interests of the children—too many early books do not take into account the changing interests of children caused by the impact of television, scientific advances and socio-economic changes. They should also realize that in the lists to which mention has been made the conflicting claims of reading, spoken and written vocabularies have not always been considered seriously enough.

The 200 basic words our reading scheme uses were selected from an analysis of children's spoken vocabulary, expressed interests, and research lists. Of course, in addition to considering which words should be included one has to consider in what order and with what frequency the words should be introduced. In writing our scheme we approached this problem of 'programming' the learning situations quite empirically. The repetition of words in reading through context was based on the needs of the majority of our school population. The mean repetition for the 200 words was 103 times, or, in

[1] E. L. Thorndike, *Teachers' Word Books of 30,000 Words* (Bureau of Publications, Teachers' College, Columbia University: New York 1944).
[2] E. Dale (ed.), 'Readability', *Elementary English*, Jan.–May, 1949.
[3] E. W. Dolch, *A Manual for Remedial Reading* (Garrard: 1945).
[4] A. E. Tansley and R. Gulliford, *The Education of Slow Learning Children* (Routledge: London 1960. Paperback edition, 1965).
[5] J. McNally and W. Murray, *Key Words to Literacy* (The Schoolmaster Publishing Co.: London 1962).
[6] G. E. R. Burroughs, *A Study of the Vocabulary of Young Children* (Oliver and Boyd: Edinburgh 1945).
[7] A. I. Gates, *A Reading Vocabulary for the Primary Grades* (Teachers' College, Columbia University: New York 1935).

other words, to learn the 200 words by sight the children read some 21,000 running words in the 16 books we used. The books have been used by children of all levels of ability during the past three years and teachers have reported that this repetition is about right for all but the very slowest learners. Bright children have responded with little help beyond being told what a word is; most average children have needed a minimum of individual word study, involving flashcards, word matching, and writing simple word-substitution and comprehension exercises.

With slower learners and children who for a variety of reasons fail to make a successful beginning to reading, a more detailed attack is necessary. Provided reading readiness has been achieved, the beginnings of reading must be capable of producing initial success and of laying the foundations for continuing progress. When the child begins to read his first book he must experience success and be motivated by a realization that he can succeed. We have found that such children need adequate preparation before tackling their first printed book. This preparation involves the teaching of the first few words he will need. Our first book contains 15 words: *a*, *and*, *blue*, *chimney*, *door*, *has*, *house*, *is*, *it*, *my*, *of*, *red*, *roof*, *the*, *window*. Some, or all, of these words are taught in the following way before the child is given Book I.

Each child has a book with pages of half-imperial sugar paper interleaved with tracing paper. On the second page the teacher prints in letters ½ in. to ¾ in. tall a sentence, say, 'My house is red.' The child memorizes this and draws a suitable picture on the opposite page. He traces the sentence with finger contact and with pencil or crayon, saying the words as he traces. If he has difficulty in recalling the sentence, individual words are studied in his own work-book. He traces the word, copies it, traces it in sand, makes it in plasticine, writes it on the blackboard, and, where appropriate, illustrates it. This is, of course, a very slow process but very few of our educationally subnormal children fail to succeed by it. When a word is recognized with reasonable certainty it is written on the child's word ladder which becomes a record of his personal sight vocabulary. It is also written in his thumb-indexed alphabet book. The sentence and the individual words are written on flashcards to ensure that the child can recognize them apart from his book. In the first place, the sentence must be written exactly as in his book. The flashcards are also used for word-word and word-picture matching exercises.

When the four words are known the process is repeated on the next page, one or two more words being introduced. The next sentence may be, 'It is a red house.' As progress is made, it becomes possible to dispense with the tracing with finger contact and to rely principally on writing, word-matching, and flashcard games. The words we use are of course comprehensible to the child—they were selected partly for this reason. Nevertheless it is important that the children should have a rich concept of the words, use them in speech in a variety of ways and thus ensure good comprehension from the beginning. For example, a discussion about houses will help the child to understand that there are many types of house within the general classification, *houses*. A discussion about the word *red* may lead to an understanding of degrees of redness. For instance, the children may be asked to bring something red to school, and these may be seriated from bright red to dull red; they may be allowed to experiment with colours to make various shades of red. This language work and experimenting not only helps in concept development and the heightening of powers of observation; it also assists word recognition and reading.

When the child knows the first fifteen words, he is allowed to read our first book called *My House*. While he is reading this, he is encouraged to do activities associated with the reading content, e.g. paint a house, make a house in plasticine or with wood, coloured blocks, or construction kits. He may also do simple comprehension exercises and have additional practice in his work-book on the words which appear to be particularly difficult for him to retain. At the same time he will be learning the new words he is to meet in the following book, using the method described earlier (our second book, called *My Garden*, introduces a further nine words: *are*, *big*, *by*, *flowers*, *garden*, *green*, *us*, *tree*, *wall*). This is an essential operation because future difficulties have to be anticipated and removed if good motivation based on continuing feelings of success is to be maintained. The preparation for the next book should also include talking about and discussing the content and thereby developing concepts of the words to be used. Thus in our scheme the teacher might talk about and discuss gardens, walls, fences, flowers, trees, big trees, big flowers and, if possible, arrange direct experiences related to gardens and gardening.

This preparation not only plays a valuable part in language development, it also ensures good comprehension and provides the child with a useful aid to word recognition—guessing by use of context clues. At this stage the child has a sight vocabulary of about 24 words. He should be encouraged to use these words in controlled and free writing as much as possible. Correct copying of the words should be insisted upon but accurate spelling should not be expected yet. The more the child reads and writes the words the better. Thus the creative teacher will introduce a variety of activities and exercises to ensure that each child sees and uses the words sufficiently for him to retain them. With very slow learners this can be difficult to achieve without boredom and frustration. With bright children such activities may be totally unnecessary and irrelevant. The procedure is then repeated for the ensuing books, with suitable modifications as learning becomes easier. Thus the teacher may dispense with the half-imperial-size tracing book, reduce the amount of individual word study and word games activity, or increase the number of comprehension exercises, free writing, and amount of associated art and craft activities, and dramatic work.

The child now begins to derive pleasure from his reading success. He responds enthusiastically to word recognition games, he matches sentences to pictures with greater ease, and enjoys the speed with which he is 'climbing' his word ladder and filling his thumb-index alphabet book. Nevertheless it is still necessary to keep a fairly tight control on his reading in order to avoid his over-reaching himself. Consequently, we only allow him to use regularly our reading scheme. However, he is not deterred from using other books incidentally and if he wants to know a word he is *told* but not at this stage *taught*. He is also surrounded by gaily illustrated, interest books and magazines and encouraged to talk about the contents. Adequate preparation for each succeeding book in the scheme is continued and the rapidly expanding sight vocabulary is used in writing, speaking and appropriate matching games. No *systematic* spelling is attempted, for reasons which will be made obvious later, but accurate copying is encouraged.

The speed with which children build up their sight vocabularies obviously varies considerably. Indeed one of the results of good individualized teaching of reading is an increasing spread of attainment in the class. This, of course, leads to organizational difficulties for the teacher who is conscious of the need to meet the individual reading needs of children. How can she cope with a large group of children whose reading abilities and attainments vary widely? The following suggestions may be of assistance.

1 The whole class need not be doing reading or reading readiness activities at any one time. Some may be reading, others can be doing art and craft or playing, provided adequate material and equipment are freely available.

2 The better readers may be allowed to help some of the weaker ones.

3 Children who are making good progress may be doing controlled or free written work. Published work-books are a useful organizational tool here, but they should be used with discrimination. Used unwisely they can result in children's progress being held back. The ideal is for the teacher to make her own graded comprehension and word study assignment cards and supplementary reading material which she uses for each child according to individual requirements.

4 If auxiliary assistance is available it is of course possible for more children to be involved in reading activities pro-

vided the qualified teacher maintains control of the programme.

5 Time-tabling may be so arranged as to allow the teacher some extra time with the slow learners.

Preparing for the use of other word recognition skills

Some children are able to continue to make progress in reading without a systematic programme for the teaching of phonics and other word recognition techniques. However, the majority of children benefit from such a programme provided it is introduced at the optimum time. Our research work, to be mentioned later, suggested that this time occurred when the child's reading age had reached about a six-and-a-half-year level on a Graded Word Reading Test. It was thus important to continue expanding the basic vocabulary by mainly visual methods until this level had been achieved. Our approach to this was quite empirical. For instance, we first chose a vocabulary of 75 words, but our Phonic Readiness Test (see later) revealed that this did not result in phonic readiness. We then increased the vocabulary to 125 words but still without the desired result. We next added a further 75 words and the total of 200 words brought the majority of children to the stage when they were ready and able to tackle a systematic programme of phonic analysis and synthesis.

The sixteen 'Racing to Read'[1] books represent our attempt at teaching the 200 words. The teacher has to keep a careful record of each child's progress in the learning of these words, and also has to be observant of the child's readiness to begin to associate individual visual symbols with particular sounds. Work on the development of auditory perception and discrimination is undertaken regularly while the visual approach is being used (see Chapter 3, section 10, for suggestions). When this work is done systematically it appears that phonic readiness can be hastened, i.e. it may be possible for phonics to be

[1] A. E. Tansley and R. H. Nichols, 'Racing to Read' (series published by E. J. Arnold and Son, Leeds).

taught even before a reading age of $6\frac{1}{2}$ years has been reached. It is as well to warn teachers, however, that it is often better to wait than to begin phonics before the child is fully competent to cope with the undoubted difficulties which phonics can entail, e.g. difficulties in auditory sequencing and blending and in discriminating between similar letter sounds, particularly those of higher sound frequencies, e.g. *s*, *th*, *ch*, *z*, *f*, *sh*.

As the child's sight vocabulary increases, he should be encouraged to discover the relationship between individual symbols or combinations of symbols and the sounds associated with them. The following activities and exercises have been found useful in achieving this:

1 When the child's alphabet-index book has sufficient words under one letter he should be asked what sound this letter makes in the appropriate words. Thus, if he has the words *big*, *boy*, *box*, *blue*, *by*, *ball* and *boat* on one page, after he has read them, or the teacher has read them to him with suitable emphasis on the initial consonant, can he independently associate '*b*' with the sound it makes? If he cannot, he is hardly likely to be ready for phonic work and needs further 'sight' reading and auditory training.

2 Show the child a picture and ask him to point out all the things or actions which begin with a given sound. 'I spy something beginning with —' is a suitable variation of this.

3 Give the child an envelope filled with pictures of a wide variety of objects, or bag of assorted articles, and ask him to classify according to the initial sound in their names. See if the child can associate the classes he makes with the written symbol for their initial sounds.

4 Repeat 3 for ending sounds and, although this is much more difficult, for middle vowel sounds and for words which rhyme.

5 See if the child can deal with inflected and derived words. For example, if he can read *run*, can he easily recognize

runs, *running*, *runner*? Reading the plurals of known words is usually easy and can be one useful way of teaching the sound 's'. Discovering the correct sound of '*ing*' is usually also comparatively easy.

6 Use published material of the 'lotto' type to encourage classifying words according to sound.

The child's response to these types of exercise and activity will provide some indication of his readiness for using a systematic programme for the teaching of phonics. However, it may be advisable to give a simple test of phonic readiness, similar to the one described in the next chapter. For teachers working in a clinical or remedial setting such a test might well be incorporated in any battery of diagnostic tests.

5 Phonic readiness and the beginnings of phonic teaching

Some general considerations

Arguments about the importance and place of phonics in the teaching of reading have been part of the general discussion about teaching techniques for generations. It is perhaps true to say that, until quite recently, the reaction against phonic instruction was due to its introduction at too early a stage. Even now, despite the introduction of well-advertised phonically biased reading schemes, many teachers favour a look-and-say and sentence approach. They have continued to maintain the position that phonic methods are too restricting in vocabulary content and, because of anomalies in the language, may lead to confusions and inaccurate reading. The introduction of new alphabets, such as the Initial Teaching Alphabet, represents an attempt to obviate the difficulties in teaching phonically irregular words, but their usefulness has not yet been reliably demonstrated by objective, long-term research. Our view has already been made clear. Research and experience have shown that with the majority of children some phonic work is necessary and beneficial. Using a Graded Word Reading Test as a guide to reading progress many teachers will have noticed that when they use a whole-word method reading ages generally improve steadily until a reading age of about 7 years is reached. A learning 'plateau' is then reached. This may in part be explained by the grading of the tests used, but it is also due to the fact that the rapid expansion of reading vocabulary needed at this stage is difficult to achieve by the use of sight methods only. This expansion can be achieved by giving the child new techniques to help word recognition when he has reached the stage in development to understand and apply them.

The abilities which appear to be desirable for the child to understand and apply phonic analysis and synthesis are:

1 *An ability to appreciate rhyme*. For instance, can the child pick out a non-rhyming word in a set of rhyming words; can he give a word which rhymes with a given word; can he choose from a list of words one which belongs to a set of rhyming words?

An ability to discriminate between letter sounds. For instance, can he cope with exercises such as:

a Which of these words begins with '*p*', '*t*', '*f*', etc.?
b Which of these words is out of place: *man*, *mother*, *cat*, *milk*, *Mary*?
c Which of these words is out of place: *mat*, *sit*, *cot*, *hut*, *fire*, *foot*?
d Which of these words is out of place: *box*, *hot*, *fight*, *lock*, *frog*?

An ability to blend sounds. A child who is unable to remember sounds in sequence and repeat them blended together rhythmically is quite unable to cope with phonics.

4 *An ability to repeat simple rhythms* such as those included in the auditory section of the perceptual programme.

5 *An ability to associate a sound with its visual representation*, either as seen or written by the child. For instance, can he cope with the following:

a Show me the letter for these sounds—'*e*', '*t*', '*g*', etc.
b Show me on this line of letters the one which says '*c*'?

A phonic readiness test

A test of phonic readiness should therefore include items to investigate all these abilities. The following is a simple test very similar to one which was used in research into phonic readiness[1] carried out by Bragg at the author's school.

Sub-test 1 *Discriminating initial sounds*

The child is asked to find the word which begins with a different sound from the others. An example is given first to ensure that the child understands what is required, e.g. Listen to these words—*Sun*, *Sand*, *Sit*, *May*; which is different? The initial sounds are slightly exaggerated in the examples given. It is suggested that the child should be told that the 'different' word may be any one of the given words.

The child is now given the following test:

Find the different word (the stranger) in these. Listen carefully.

1	Go	girl	top	gate
2	Top	cup	tin	tie
3	Sugar	down	shape	shilling
4	Fly	cloth	climb	clock
5	Green	grey	ground	count
6	Face	fairy	room	fall
7	Rabbit	hill	rich	robin
8	Nut	nice	nail	lid
9	match	meat	name	man
10	Thief	thick	foot	thank

Sub-test 2 *Discriminating rhyming words*

The administration is similar to that for sub-test 1. A nursery rhyme may be used to illustrate the meaning of rhyme.

[1] H. Bragg, 'Readiness for Phonics in Dull Children', *Special Education*, vol. LI, no. 2, 1962.

Demonstration item: bat, rat, cat, brick.

1	fall	run	ball	wall
2	heel	steel	bell	wheel
3	bat	boat	coat	goat
4	round	horse	found	sound
5	tin	ten	pin	win
6	keep	sheep	tape	weep
7	new	low	sow	go
8	gain	main	rain	mate
9	night	safe	sight	kite
10	fun	foot	gun	run

Sub-test 3 *Blending*

The child is asked to listen to sounds given at about one per second. For example, listen to these sounds: '*a*', '*t*'. Put them together—what word do they make when put together? Care must be taken to give the sound as accurately as possible.

1	g	o		6	s	i	t
2	u	s		7	b	i	g
3	m	e		8	e	n	d
4	c	a	t	9	ch	ur	ch
5	m	a	p	10	br	i	ck

Sub-test 4 *Association of visual and auditory symbols*

For this test, the Morris Game[1] was used. The child is shown two cards each having four pictures on it: each picture on a card begins with the same sound. On the back of the card the appropriate initial letter is given but this is not pointed out to the child. The child has to pick the correct card when a picture is named, the cards being shuffled out of sight of the testee.

[1] R. Morris, *The Quality of Learning* (Methuen: London 1951).

This test is designed to explore the child's ability to associate a sound with its visual presentation and vice versa.

The child's ability to cope with phonic synthesis was assessed by asking the child to blend visually presented nonsense words such as the following:

a m p	h o r
e f f	l a n g
b o d	n a s t
c u g	p r o t
d e p	a d o n
f i m	a r o c k
g a n	h a v i s
j e b	l o t e
m a l	e l l i n g
k u t	d e l l o w

Results and indications

In the first three sub-tests one mark was awarded for each correct answer. Bragg found that scores 14 to 17 appeared to indicate satisfactory readiness for a phonic approach. He also found that a score of 4 or 5 on each test is necessary as a true indication of readiness.

The research population was small (N = 30) and all were educationally subnormal, but the following correlations were found:

	Phonic readiness as assessed
Chronological age	0·02
Mental Age (Binet)	0·43
Reading Age (Graded Word)	0·74 (significant at 1 per cent level)

These correlations appear to support the thesis already given that phonic readiness should be viewed more in relation to reading age and early reading experiences than to mental maturity *per se*. Long experience also suggests that this is applicable to most children although there will be many individual exceptions.

The beginnings of phonic teaching

Some general principles

1 Before beginning phonic instruction, readiness must have been firmly established by adequate sight reading and practice in auditory perception and discrimination.

2 Where possible, the study of phonograms should begin by study of words already known by sight or by using words included in sentences which help the child to make intelligent guesses from context clues.

3 Teach phonics as part of language development and not as an isolated skill. Thus, new phonically regular words which have been learned should immediately be incorporated in reading for comprehension and pleasure, and be used in free and controlled writing and spelling. The child then appreciates the use of what he has learned and is encouraged by success.

4 Introduce new learning situations with due regard to level of difficulty and in such a way as to encourage the child to learn independently at his own level and with good motivation based on continuing feelings of success.

5 Drill is perhaps essential but it should be purposeful and serve as revision and consolidation of work previously completed with understanding.

6 Combine phonic work with plenty of oral work, free writing and the teaching of systematic spelling related to the phonic programme.

7 Supplement the phonic teaching with a varied, well-graded supply of supplementary reading, and comprehension work.

8 Make due allowances for the individual differences in the children. In general, the 'programming' of learning situations should be such as to meet the learning needs of the slowest child in the group. In books, such as the 'Sound Sense'[1] books, this is of course almost impossible. The good teacher will, therefore, have to adjust the grading of work according to needs. Slower learners will need more varied presentations of new learning to enable them to make abstractions and generalizations and will need more consolidation exercises and repetition. Quicker learners will not need all the exercises in the published books. If the teacher is certain that a specific piece of learning is thoroughly understood by the child, then new learning should be introduced. This obviates boredom and ensures that the child is making progress more or less at his own rate.

   This approach to organizing teaching leads to individualization of treatment. However, some group work should be undertaken with children who are at similar levels of reading development. Good readers should be given opportunities to help weaker ones.

9 An over-emphasis on phonics should be avoided and children should be encouraged to make use of other techniques to 'unlock' words which are difficult. The use of context clues should be particularly stressed.

10 As a general rule, in the early stages of phonic learning a child should be able to blend sounds orally before they are presented to him visually. Experienced teachers will be aware of the difficulties which backward children display in blending. Such children are often confused because letters have names and also represent sounds. They also have poor auditory memories and are often handicapped by lack of rhythm. They therefore need training in these together with activities and methods such as the following:

[1] A series of eight books by A. E. Tansley, published by E. J. Arnold and Son, Leeds.

a Using visuo-motor methods of word study saying words as they are written, or traced in writing with finger contact.

b Decreasing the vocalization of words. Some children show marked improvement when they are encouraged to whisper words or to lip-read words given by the teacher.

c Paying particular attention to the correct production of sounds and using a mirror to look at the position of tongue and lips.

d Using flashcards of phonic elements.

e Blending sounds by using tonality—e.g. joining two sounds by changing intonation as the sounds are joined together.

f Using tape recorders or play-back machines in conjunction with individual work sheets.

g Paying particular attention to pronunciation units in known words and finding them in words which the child cannot read, e.g. '*ing*' in *sing, ring, thing, swimming*, or '*old*' in *cold*, *sold*, *told*, *bold*, *hold*, etc.

h Paying particular attention to initial sounds and to the order of sounds in spoken words.

11 New sounds should be learned according to level of difficulty and due regard should be given to the frequency of the sound in reading and spoken language.

12 The systematic programme of phonic instruction should be abandoned as soon as the child is sufficiently competent in word recognition to manage without it.

13 As the child's phonic ability increases he will be capable of reading many words which are meaningless to him. In the later stages of the programme, therefore, it is necessary to concentrate on word study, comprehension, and the development of concepts by discussion, and by simple research undertaken by the child himself with teacher guidance.

6 The teaching of phonics

Introduction

There are, of course, several ways of teaching phonic analysis. For example, the study of long lists of phonically regular words as part of reading, or as something separate from the reading lesson; the teaching of phonics incidentally to sight reading by giving the child help with unknown phonograms whenever they are required and irrespective of level of difficulty. Our method,[1] based on the principles given at the end of the previous chapter, is designed to teach phonics as an integral part of language development. It therefore involves speaking, listening, controlled and free written expression, spelling, mechanical reading and comprehension, and controlled supplementary reading for information and pleasure, and leads the child to higher levels of reading and language development.

What has therefore evolved from our work is a language scheme with a phonic bias, involving word study, simple grammar, comprehension exercises and related spelling. The introduction of the different sounds and phonic elements has been based on a compromise between frequency in reading

[1] A. E. Tansley, 'Sound Sense' (series published by E. J. Arnold and Son, Leeds).

and spoken vocabularies and learning difficulty. The frequency was assessed by reference to the word lists mentioned in Chapter 4, and difficulty of learning was based on the observations of teachers with long experience in the teaching of reading and in dealing with backward children.

In order to maintain good motivation and provide for adequate grading, consolidation and revision, a wide variety of exercises was used. These exercises included the following:

1 Putting words into *sound* families.

2 Finding from given lists words which belong to a given sound family.

3 Spontaneous giving of words belonging to a given family.

4 Finding the stranger in a given list of words.

5 Putting in missing sounds.

6 Joining with a line words beginning or ending with the same sound.

7 Rearranging jumbled words into sentences.

8 Rearranging jumbled sentences into a meaningful passage.

9 Choosing the sight word from several alternatives or given lists.

10 Sentence completion.

11 Story completion.

12 Make up words from given letters.

13 Finding words within words.

14 Adding digraphs to the beginning or ending of given phonograms or pronunciation units.

15 Word sums.

16 Finding words which rhyme or finding the stranger in a list of rhyming words.

17 Exercises on words which belong to various classes, e.g. occupations, food, drink, nationalities, materials, colours, etc.

18 Finding answers to given questions.

19 Making up questions to given answers.

20 Exercises on plurality, comparatives, superlatives and opposites.

21 Finding right and wrong statements.

22 Reading short passages and stories and answering comprehension questions of varying degrees of difficulty.

23 Drawing pictures or making simple models from written instructions.

24 Suffixes and prefixes together with inflected and derived forms of given words.

25 Word squares and simple crosswords.

26 Word puzzles, e.g. *I have four legs, I am a pet, I go bow-wow, what am I?*

27 Writing a story with key words given.

28 Giving words for given definitions and vice versa.

29 Dictionary work.

30 Changing tenses of given sentences.

As stated earlier, before a systematic phonic programme is started the children have already learned the common consonants and have had some limited experience in the structural analysis of words, e.g. finding pronunciation units in words, adding sounds to known words, compounding known words into new ones. The phonic programme proper begins with the learning of the five short vowel sounds—*a*, *i*, *o*, *u*, *e*—in the order given. Each sound is first introduced as it occurs in words known by sight; for example, the *a* sound in *am*, *and*, *at*, *as*, *ask*, *back*, *black*, *cat*, etc. The child should be asked to listen to the '*a*' sound in the words and also to select other words in his sight vocabulary which have the *a* sound in them. He should then be introduced to new three-letter words with *a* in them. The sounds are given in isolation first, e.g. *m a t*, and the child repeats them as an auditory memory exercise. He is then taught to say the sounds more and more quickly to instil the idea of *blending*. This process is facilitated more quickly if sounds such as *m*, *n*, *s*, *f*, *l*, are used as initial sounds since these blend more readily than others. It seems important that the child should be able to listen to the sounds and to blend smoothly before the visual symbols are introduced. However, once symbols are used, writing the word should be used to provide kinaesthetic reinforcement. The child should be encouraged to say the word, as a whole, as he writes it. This helps to obviate too much emphasis on individual elements in the word and also faulty pronunciation such as *cu-a-tu* for *cat*. It also encourages better eye-movements and blending.

The ability to remember sounds in sequence and to blend them smoothly and rhythmically into words is so fundamental to successful progress in developmental reading that teachers must ensure that the skill is thoroughly acquired. If the child appears completely unable to blend, then training in auditory perception must be continued. If the child shows readiness for phonics but finds blending particularly difficult, then systematic, well-graded teaching has to be used until success is achieved. This teaching will have to incorporate some of the following:

1 More training in associating the required sound with its visual symbol. This is often difficult for backward children who have difficulty in appreciating that letters have an alphabetical name and also represent sounds. They tend to persist in using the name. The teaching of the *sounds* of common consonants and vowels is an essential beginning to a phonic programme.

2 Training in blending two sounds into known or nonsense words. In extreme cases of difficulty, speaking and tracing

the letters with finger contact is necessary. The two sounds may be written on cards; the cards are placed about two feet apart and the child says the sounds separately. The cards are moved together gradually and the child is encouraged to say the sounds more and more quickly as the cards are brought closer together.

3 There is often argument concerning whether initial or final blends should be used. In practice, most teachers use both techniques. For instance, when pronunciation or meaning units are used for blending, initial blends can be employed; for example, '*ing*' may be blended with *s*, *r*, *k* to make *sing*, *ring* and *king*; '*and*' may be blended with *b*, *l*, *s*, *h* to make *band*, *land*, *sand*, *hand*, etc., etc. When plurals, participles and derived words are used final blending has to be used, e.g. as in run*s*, runn*ing*, runn*er*.

4 With backward children it is sometimes recommended that individual sounds in words should be sounded separately and not blended in pairs either initially or finally. Thus in studying the word *ran* the children should sound out *r-a-n* and not be taught *ra-n* or *r-an*. Our experience is that with certain children this is helpful. However, we generally find that if the child knows *an* then he learns fairly quickly how to precede *an* with the *r* sound. Words which do not have known words within them are perhaps better taught as being made up of separate sounds—thus *not* is taught as *n-o-t* to be blended. Nevertheless it is impossible to be dogmatic because there are individual differences. The good teacher soon appreciates which technique is best suited to each child.

5 The introduction of new sounds must be carefully controlled. Any new word met in reading which includes sounds not already known should be dealt with as a new sight word.

6 Good motivation must be maintained despite learning difficulty. Play situations should be devised, e.g. finding letters for given sounds when blindfolded (the letters may

be made out of sandpaper or sand sprinkled on glue), fishing for sounds, playing Sound Snap (the teacher gives the sound and the children search for the card with the correct letter on it), finding a sound to make a given sound into a word, lip-reading a word and finding letters to make it. We have also found that some children benefit from using a tape play-back with prepared work sheets for the tape.

A reading scheme

The order in which sounds are introduced into a systematic programme for teaching phonic analysis must be flexible to meet the needs of individual children. In the eight books we use, the sounds are introduced as follows:

BOOK 1 a i o u e short vowel sounds
2 ee oo
3 long a, i, o with final e
4 ar er or all
5 sh st th (2 sounds) ch
6 wh bl tr dr fr gr fl cl, final **y** (as in fly and baby) ea (as in tea and dead)
7 ai ay, oi oy, ou, ow (2 sounds), oa, au aw
8 igh, er ur ir, ew, ge dge, air are, ie (2 sounds), -tion -ation -ection, sion, ph, kn, gn, wr, hard and soft c

We make no claim that this order is correct, but it appears to satisfy the two criteria we used in selection, viz., frequency in language and difficulty in learning. Ten years' experience of using the scheme indicates that from a reading age of 6½ years for Book 1, reading improves comparatively evenly to an average reading age of 10½ years for the 250 children who have completed Book 8. A study of the reading progress of some 150 children, all of whom were educationally subnormal and some also maladjusted, has shown that over a period of 3 years (and in some cases 4 and 5 years) the mean gain in mechanical reading age has been about 10½ months per year per child. Considering that the group included severely disturbed, 'brain-injured', and some low-grade children, this result seems to suggest that the reading scheme used is very successful and is closely related to development in reading skills. Comparable figures are not available for a 'normal' population but average yearly increments of reading age of more than 12 months should be expected on the above evidence.

The study also demonstrated another very important fact—results on the Neale Analysis of Reading Ability,[1] which gives scores for Reading Accuracy, Speed, and Comprehension, showed similar gains on all three aspects of reading. It seems therefore that the reading scheme, together with the language programme of which it is part, does lead to all-round psycholinguistic improvements. It is, of course, impossible to say whether the scheme is based on a sound model of the psycholinguistic processes involved in reading. Improvements could have resulted from a number of factors, e.g. systematic teaching and emphasis on programming, or good motivation arising out of the children's knowing that the scheme originated in their school and that many visitors came to see them. Nevertheless, the evidence suggests that a reading scheme which is based on the principles listed in Chapter 1 does give encouraging results.

Supplementary activities

1 Supplementary reading

The phonic scheme as represented in the 'Sound Sense' books is only the skeleton around which the total reading and language programme is built. The controlled use of supplementary reading is essential to give consolidation and repetition, to help the child to get information and pleasure out of his developing reading skill, and to improve linguistic com-

[1] M. D. Neale, *Neale Analysis of Reading Ability* (Macmillan: London 1958).

munication totally. The eight books in our scheme have been found over a number of years to result in graded word reading ages as follows:

BOOK 1	6 –6½ years		BOOK 5	8 –8½ years
2	6½–7 years		6	8½–9 years
3	7 –7½ years		7	9 –9½ years
4	7½–8 years		8	9½–10½ years

It will be seen, therefore, that the scheme does produce a continuing, uniform development in reading skills. Of course, other schemes, provided they are well-graded and applied systematically, may produce similar or better results.

The above reading ages, given as a guide to supplementary reading, are only useful to teachers who know how to assess the level of reading difficulty in children's books. This assessment is not difficult for teachers who have been trained in the use of reading tests. If the hardest words on three or four pages of a book are related to the grading in a word recognition test the reading level of the book can be assessed fairly accurately. Sentence length and construction, and the degree of concreteness or abstractness in expression may also have to be borne in mind.

The following aspects of supplementary reading material must also be considered:

1 The material selected must have breadth, as well as grading. For slow-learning children in particular, many books at a given reading level must be available in order to ensure adequate consolidation, repetition and revision of phonic elements learned.

2 The material at each level must be related to the interests of the children. It must therefore include stories about interesting people, things and situations. It must also serve to stimulate curiosity and develop new interests.

3 The reading material must at all levels, and particularly at higher levels, encourage the development of comprehension and concepts.

4 The material must be freely accessible to the children and displayed in an attractive way.

5 It must be displayed in such a way that the children know which books are appropriate for them. In the author's school, the reading age is put in each book and the books are arranged, in order of reading difficulty, on shelves around the classroom. The children are told their reading ages and they are instructed how to choose suitable reading books. They soon learn that if they want to read for pleasure they have to choose books at or slightly below their own reading ages.

6 The word 'supplementary' has been used to indicate reading which is closely related to the child's improving phonic ability and increasing reading age. Some of the supplementary reading may have to be controlled, particularly in the earlier stages of phonic teaching when grading and consolidation are important. Certain supplementary readers may therefore become *basic readers*, particularly for slow learners. No one scheme need be adhered to once the basic sight vocabulary has been learned and phonic readiness firmly established. Selected books from several schemes may be used, at all levels, provided they give adequate practice in the phonic elements being taught. The teacher's concern, at all times, should be the development of a *thoroughly systematic*, well-programmed scheme of reading.

2 *Supplementary writing and spelling*

1 Free writing should be encouraged throughout. This should be supported by comprehension work and 'controlled' writing as in factual descriptions of people, things and scenes, in imaginary stories, and in simple verse.

2 Systematic spelling should be taught when systematic phonic analysis starts and should be closely related to the phonic programme.

3 *Supplementary listening*

There are two important aspects of language in communication, namely, the receptive and expressive. There is perhaps, in schools a lack of balance between the two; yet both are of great importance and interrelated. Those teachers who deal with backward children or children suffering from expressive or receptive aphasias are well aware of the disastrous effects of lack of balance between these two elements in psycholinguistic development. A deficiency in either retards the development of the other and leads to retardation in all aspects of language function. Supplementary activity must therefore include many opportunities for teaching children how to listen. This is certainly of great importance in teaching slow learners.

The supplementary activities should therefore provide opportunities for listening to directions, environmental sounds, music, talks by adults and children, poetry, and above all, a variety of stories. Such opportunities reinforce the expressive side of language and help the child to become interested in words and sentences.

4 *Supplementary oral work*

This arises naturally from individual reading and good listening. In oral expression the child should be encouraged to ask questions freely, to enunciate clearly, to speak loudly enough and with voice modulation, and to sing as well as possible. The place of dramatic activity, particularly of a creative and spontaneous kind, should not be forgotten. Choral verse speaking is also useful. This is not the place to give detailed suggestions as to how to stimulate good oral expression. However, good teachers will organize activities and experiences and provide many opportunities to encourage children in the skilful use of oral language.

All these supplementary activities encourage reading development and lead to significant improvements in phonic ability. More importantly, they are essential for good language communication.

The teaching of spelling

As stated earlier, in our language programme the systematic teaching of spelling is begun when the teaching of phonics begins. This seems the obvious time to begin because the writing and correct spelling of words are additional aids to phonics. Thus, when the child is learning to read words including the short vowel sounds, he learns to write them correctly from memory and to use them in written expression. The method used in teaching spelling should reinforce the method used in the teaching of reading. It should take into account the individual differences in the class and should play its part in developing those abilities being used in the reading process. In our programme, therefore, the spelling method has to foster the development of phonic analysis and blending and also lead to improvements in the receptive and expressive sides of language.

Individual differences

Any class of children, even in large streamed schools, will have a wide range of spelling ability and attainments. Class teaching is therefore bound to be inefficient; individual or group teaching must be used. The size of the groups will have to be related to the spread of attainments and to the teacher's skill as an organizer. In the writer's school, however, the children work in pairs and this does not appear to create difficulty for the teachers. It is, of course, impossible to teach each pair in a single lesson, but a flexible approach to time-tabling allows children to do other activities when they are in need of help. Furthermore, arrangements allow good spellers to assist poor ones and the grading of work is such that to a great extent the children are able to work independently.

Differences in ability make it necessary to use several modes of perceiving words; the teaching method therefore uses visual, auditory, kinaesthetic (speaking and writing) and, when necessary, tactile approaches. Thus, with children who have special difficulty because of visuo-motor or visuo-spatial disturbance (as shown in tendencies to reversals and directional confusion), tracing the word with finger contact has to be used; with children who have poor memories for auditory sequences, attention should be drawn to the visuo/auditory relationships in phonically regular words; children with poor visual perception should be given extra help in copying and remembering phonically irregular words. There are some children who are particularly good spellers who do not require systematic teaching in spelling. Some of these children need help in understanding words and in using them in written expression. They consequently need dictionary exercises, help in the making of definitions, and additional comprehension work.

A suggested method

1 The teachers prepare a set of graded assignments, each of not more than fifteen words. Books of assignments are available but we use the 110 assignments given in the 'Sound Sense' Teacher's Book[1] because these are related to our phonic programme. The assignments must include phonically irregular words in common usage and make adequate provision for repetition and revision.

[1] A. E. Tansley, *Teacher's Handbook* to 'Sound Sense' Series.

2 The class is given a standardized spelling test and the children are grouped in pairs according to attainment level.

3 Each pair is given the assignment which matches or is just below its spelling level. Teachers who are experienced in the use of standardized tests will be able to assess levels of difficulty within reasonable limits. In any case, the levels may be fixed empirically.

4 The assignments are copied in the child's handwriting and the teacher ensures that the copy is correct and that the child can read and pronounce each word accurately and clearly.

5 The children now study the words in their assignment in the following way:

a The two children study the assignment independently; they look at a word, say it and try to memorize its visual form; without looking at the word they try to write it, and then check their attempt against the correct spelling. This procedure is repeated until the word is known. Each word in the assignment is studied in the same way.

b When they have studied every word they test each other; a word is given and the child writes the word, saying it as he writes. (In saying the word the child should say it slowly in its entirety, not letter by letter, or sound by sound.) Oral recall is not encouraged because spelling is needed principally in writing and depends on visual, auditory and kinaesthetic memories. The spelling is then checked by the partner.

c When the two children are confident about their ability to spell every word in the assignment, they ask the teacher to test them. The teacher asks them to spell all, or selected, words in the assignment.

d The teacher, when satisfied, asks each child to write sentences which illustrate the meaning of selected words, or gives previously prepared comprehension exercises. Oral sentences may be accepted where appropriate. It should be stressed here that motivation should not be harmed by too rigid an insistence on this part of the teaching method. If the children can obviously use the words they have learned to spell in communication, they should not be held back.

e The above method is now repeated on the next assignment.

In using the assignment technique it is important for the teacher to maintain good motivation the whole time. The grading of the complete assignments should be such that the slowest learners experience cumulative feelings of success. Quicker learners will not therefore need to work all the assignments in full.

We have previously stressed the importance of encouraging creative writing as a fundamental part of the reading and language programmes. When marking free compositions correct only those spelling mistakes which the child at his spelling attainment level ought not to make. Too many corrections may greatly inhibit a child's willingness to express himself freely, unselfconsciously and pleasurably.

8 Reading failure: its causes and prevention

Despite the improvement in reading standards in recent years there are still many children who find reading difficult and who leave school with attainments too low for reading to be a useful and pleasurable activity. These failing children have great difficulty in developing healthy attitudes towards themselves and others; they either isolate themselves from social contacts and become withdrawn and depressed or, in order to compensate for feelings of inadequacy, become aggressive, uncooperative, unreliable, pleasure-seeking and, perhaps, delinquent. It is well known that the incidence of reading backwardness is much higher in delinquents than in the population as a whole. Whatever the causal relationships, teachers who work with delinquents and emotionally disturbed children know that dramatic improvements in behaviour often occur with improvements in reading. The causes of failure may be difficult to determine, the relationship between causes and symptoms may be obscure, but the results of failure are usually obvious. Without success in reading, educational progress in general will be retarded. Teachers must therefore be cognizant at all times of their obligation to prevent reading backwardness if possible, and to treat it with all the skill and understanding they can muster when it arises.

The causes of reading failure

Many causative factors may be involved in failure to read and seldom is one factor solely responsible. We cannot list and discuss all the possible factors, and combinations of factors here. However, there are some which are so important as to warrant mention. These are:

1 Lack of knowledge by teachers of the developmental processes involved in the acquisition of reading skills. Teachers have tended to teach reading by empirical, trial-and-error methods rather than by basing their methods and techniques on the developing abilities which are involved in the reading process. One outcome of this has been a proliferation of methods and a lack of system in organizing reading programmes.

2 A lack of awareness of the influence on learning of individual differences in children arising not only from differences in intellectual endowment but from variations in personality, socio-economic backgrounds, and cultural levels. Research has tended to show that social and environmental factors can be more important in relation to reading failure than lack of intelligence as indicated by low intelligence test scores. The research of Malmquist[1] into reading failure in Swedish first-grade children showed, for instance, that:

   a The mean I.Q. for poor readers was 96·62 compared with 107·9 for the whole sample.
   b 36 per cent of poor readers had an I.Q. of 100+; 64 per cent had an I.Q. of 90+.
   c There was a significant relationship between social group and the child's reading ability. The following were significantly related to reading level: joint taxable income of parents, father's education, mother's education, social status of parents, numbers of books in the

[1] Malmquist, *Reading Disabilities in the First Grade of the Elementary School* (Almquist and Wiksell: Stockholm 1958).

home and in the child's own room, size of dwelling, and the child's disposal of a room for himself.

d Premature birth, speech defects, and disturbed visual perception (see Chapter 3) were also found to have great significance.

The same research showed a significant relationship between certain personality traits and reading disability, but how far these traits were the cause or result of failure is difficult to assess.

Other research workers have found similar relationships; the findings of Ginsberg and Bray[1] are particularly interesting. They found, not surprisingly, that educational failure rates varied considerably in different American regions and states. In their study of men who were rejected on grounds of 'mental deficiency' for military service in World War II they found:

a Rejections from S.E. regions were ten times as high as those from the Far West.

b Rejections of negroes were six times rejections of whites.

c Rejections of whites in S.E. and S.W. were greater than for negroes in the N.W. and Far West.

d Rejections varied from 0·9 per cent of whites in Far West to 20 per cent of negroes in the S.E.

e Rejections varied according to financial appropriations for education.

Teachers in this country know only too well that the great majority of backward readers come from the poorer families and lower socio-economic groups. It can be argued that they are backward because their parents are poor due to low intelligence and that heredity makes them of low intelligence too. However, there is now sufficient evidence to throw serious doubts on this argument. We must not confuse biological inheritance and social inheritance, nor should we assume that they are closely associated until indisputable supportive evidence can be evinced.

[1] E. Ginsberg and D. W. Bray, *The Uneducated* (Columbia University Press: New York 1953).

3 Lack of awareness that reading, particularly mechanical reading, has a neurological basis and that reading success is unattainable until a certain level of neurological development has been reached. Signs of neurological immaturity or abnormality, as evidenced by poor muscular co-ordination, speech defects, perceptual disturbance, and inadequate cerebral dominance, are often observed in children who have or had reading disabilities.

4 Insufficient awareness on the part of parents and some teachers of the importance of learning readiness and of the damage to emotional development and later learning that results from introducing children to learning situations which they are too immature to meet.

5 Failure to appreciate the need for praise and encouragement and good motivation at all times. A child's learning efficiency depends upon his emotional state when learning takes place or is expected. If, because of repeated failure and frustration, the child becomes emotionally disorganized and fearful, his future will to learn will be greatly inhibited by poor concentration and lack of motivation and perseverance. Teachers of backward and maladjusted pupils regularly meet children who are so frustrated, ashamed and lacking in confidence that they have developed defensive reactions and neurotic conditions.

6 Poor and inappropriate teaching which has resulted from inadequate teacher training. All teacher trainees, even those preferring to teach in Secondary Schools, should be trained in the teaching of all aspects of reading. Even if they never have to teach a child to read, they will derive benefit from learning about the application of developmental psychology and programmed learning to the acquisition of reading skills.

What can be done to prevent reading failure?

Failure in reading is due to a variety of causes which are always interrelated and interdependent. The failure may be due to a combination of inherited, congenital, physical, emotional, or environmental factors, but the relationship between them is never easy to determine, particularly in children who have been failing for a long time. With them the original causes often become overlaid by acquired symptoms. Thus, failure may be ascribed to poor intellectual endowment, e.g. as indicated by a low I.Q.; however, we have already stressed that a low I.Q. is no certain indication of poor biological inheritance. There is, of course, abundant evidence in research to confirm that a poor biological inheritance is generally worsened by any physical or sensory handicap, emotional disturbance or deprived environment. Again, failure may be due to organic causes—mild cerebral dysfunction is likely to result in psychomotor disability, perceptual disturbance, aphasias, attentional defects, personality deviations, and environmental difficulties due to consequent mismanagement and lack of understanding. In such cases, it is often impossible to determine to what extent the failure to read is due to the brain damage *per se* or to the psychological and environmental *sequelae* of it. Yet again, failure may be due to emotional disturbance caused by too hasty an introduction to reading by over-ambitious parents or teachers; here the child may set up defences against learning to read, display psychosomatic conditions, show deterioration in intelligence test scores, and become progressively more difficult to motivate.

It is thus often difficult to isolate causes and to differentiate between causes, effects and symptoms. Teachers working in a normal school setting may therefore feel that much time would be wasted in attempting to diagnose causes before they begin to take remedial steps. In any case, few teachers are at present sufficiently well trained to attempt a comprehensive diagnosis let alone relate scientific treatment to it. Consequently, they approach the problem empirically andtoften achieve surprisingly good results. However, their m thods usually constitute nothing more than intensive syseematic coaching using well-tried methods and reading schemes, such as those mentioned earlier. Much of what is described as remedial work is nothing more than this. Of course this coaching is valuable and doubtless prevents much ultimate backwardness.

These teachers should realize, however, that in many cases the treatment they give is what may be described as *peripheral* rather than *fundamental* or *basic*. They might find it helpful to think in terms of two types of backwardness: pseudo or conditioned backwardness due to environmental and psychogenic factors, and real backwardness caused by aetiological factors such as brain injury, sensory deficiencies, markedly inferior intelligence, mental disorder or other pathological conditions.

These two types or classes of backwardness cannot, of course, be differentiated absolutely nor can their degree be reliably measured except in terms of chronological age. However, the concept of pseudo-backwardness is a useful one in that treatment becomes primarily concerned with manipulating the environment to organize success and good motivation. A detailed diagnosis of backwardness may in such cases be unnecessary because success may result from systematic coaching based on good teacher-child relationship. However, some measure of *present* intellectual status is generally desirable in order to avoid over-optimism. One danger inherent in making an assessment of intelligence is that a mental age may be used to set the upper limit of reading attainment or to assess readiness. There is now sufficient research evidence, and our own experience over the past fifteen years supports this, to raise serious doubts about the predictive value of mental ages as indicators of optimum levels of attainment, particularly in reading, and especially in relation to children with severe reading disability. The variation of abilities within the individual, which are masked by any global assessment or measure such as an I.Q., can also often upset any prediction of success or failure. For example, a child with a low I.Q. may well possess abilities which make good levels of reading quite possible. This is often seen in some educationally subnormal children who find mechanical reading quite easy.

When intensive coaching fails to produce results the teacher may be faced with true or real backwardness which is more intractable. A thorough, comprehensive diagnosis then becomes essential. (See later chapters.) Nevertheless, there is now mounting evidence that even this backwardness can be limited in severity by early diagnosis and scientific, systematic, related remedial treatment. The degree of backwardness and its exacerbation by faulty or delayed treatment can be progressively reduced.

The above discussion indicates that every effort should be made, particularly in the earlier stages of children's education, to prevent backwardness and reduce its many serious effects. This effort should be based on the following considerations:

1 Poor linguistic backgrounds

Attempts must be made to ameliorate the disadvantages of language deprivation resulting from poor linguistic backgrounds. Special attention must be given to providing stimulating experiences of a broad and varied character. Thus, in the case of immigrant children, no real progress in reading is likely to be made until they have become conversant with our language and culture. A reading readiness programme for them must include many explorations of the environment and ample opportunities for talk and discussion. Without these, the books we use can be rather meaningless, and reading may be good mechanically but poor in comprehension. These children need also play experiences with the materials used by children in our culture so that they have the same opportunities for the adequate development of those sensori-motor skills, constructive abilities, and perceptual and conceptual processes needed for learning in our educational system. We have met coloured children whose language development was so poor that they were quite unable to pin concepts to words they were able to read mechanically.

Of course, many British children suffer under similar handicaps; indeed, it is often difficult for teachers from middle-class backgrounds to appreciate how little communication exists in the homes of some deprived children. The 'average' child of six should have a spoken vocabulary of 6,000–7,000 words; many backward children of six have spoken vocabularies of 1,000–

2,000 words or less. They therefore have great difficulty in understanding the language they hear from other children and teachers, and if they are able to read, are unable to comprehend and to have rich concepts. They are still further handicapped because they have even less awareness of the meaning and use of words which are vital in the development of relational thinking, e.g. prepositions, adverbs and adjectives. They therefore find it difficult to make abstractions from and generalizations about their environment. *They are unable to learn how to learn.*

Many backward children have had little contact with books, periodicals, magazines or newspapers. The school must therefore remedy the deficiency by surrounding the child with these media of communication. Looking at well-illustrated books will do much to stimulate a desire to communicate, to become curious and interested in things, and to seek and exchange information and ideas.

2 *School organization*

Teachers must not only be made aware of the psychology of individual differences; they must also receive training in how to organize their teaching to tackle the educational problems created by these differences. It seems that few colleges of education make any serious attempt to show students how to arrange their teaching so that they are capable of making some attempt at providing each child with an education suited to its age, ability and aptitude. There is, of course, some value in showing students how to prepare, plan and present a set lesson and, in the first place, such a lesson may have to be given to a whole class. A little experience of *class* teaching soon demonstrates to the sensitive teacher its inefficiency and inadequacy. Post-lesson tests will clearly indicate that the response of the children varies considerably and this obtains no matter what the age or intellectual status of the class may be. The good, well-trained teacher must therefore be capable of dividing her class into groups of convenient size, of carrying on several 'lessons' simultaneously, of remaining flexible in the methods and curriculum she uses, and of providing learning situations which are tailored to the psychological and educational needs of every child. This is perhaps asking too much of teachers, particularly at present when class sizes are much too large. However, it should be stressed in order to make teachers appreciate that *class* or *mass* teaching should be anathema to them.

The exponents of streaming will, of course, put forward the plea that they believe in streaming because it helps teachers to deal more adequately with a more limited range of individual difference. However, even in large schools where streaming might be expected to result in groups which are fairly homogeneous for learning purposes, a detailed look at the children will reveal a very wide range in learning ability, to say nothing of differences in personality, backgrounds, interests and emotional and social development. In the author's school which caters for educationally subnormal pupils who have been screened for low intelligence, a comprehensive survey has clearly shown that the population in it is as heterogeneous as that found in any group. The children have been examined medically, neurologically, psychologically and educationally, and family and case histories have been completed for each child. The data obtained have shown that each child is different and presents a 'unique' individual educational experiment. We are certain that a similar result would be found for any group of children irrespective of age, class or school. For example, an analysis of children in an 'A' stream in a large grammar school would yield similar results and indicate the inefficiency of much of the subject-centred teaching that prevails.

To prevent backwardness, therefore, schools must be prepared to examine not only their methods but also their organization. Since the main attack on prevention of reading failure must be made in the Primary School let us briefly examine what changes might be tried. Some schools have already made changes and are engaged in exciting experiments.

First, we should think about using more flexible systems of grouping children. The class system is often applied very rigidly and a child, once placed in a class, tends to remain in it for far too long. An organization based on cross-classification or 'setting' for various subjects or groups of subjects might be tried. This system can be very flexible and allow children to move across 'sets' as the speed and depth of their learning change. Again, some schools have experimented with so-called family groupings. In this, children may be grouped in 'families' which cover the whole or part of the age-range of the Primary School and ignore attainments and intelligence ratings. This has obvious social benefits but it could also lead to improvements in attainments, particularly if it were supplemented by cross-classification, and special groupings for remedial work.

The evidence for and against streaming is not yet sufficient to lead to reliable conclusions. Statements have been made that unstreaming reduces the incidence of backwardness without detriment to brighter children. My own school is unstreamed and the evidence suggests:

1 There has been no deterioration in the attainment gains made by brighter children in basic subjects.

2 The failing children, and particular older ones, have gained in confidence and social status and in most cases have been helped by their more successful friends.

3 Children with acute learning difficulties have been more strongly motivated to accept and benefit from remedial help.

4 Teachers have had to individualize treatment. They have therefore gained knowledge and experience in handling a wider range of learning problems and their teaching has become more systematic and inspiring.

5 With the desegregation of the slowest learners all teachers have become more aware of the needs of these children and have made greater efforts on their behalf.

6 Children with marked reading disability have needed extra help.

All Primary Schools should have at least one teacher who has been thoroughly trained in the diagnosis and treatment of reading disability. Large schools should have a Remedial Department to give special, systematic help to poor readers either within their own class or grouping, or in specially arranged reading classes. For extremely difficult cases of reading failure, the remedial teaching staff should be helped and guided by the school psychological service working *in the school* and playing its part not only in diagnosis but also in treatment. The present arrangement whereby children are sent out of schools to a clinic is usually inefficient for the following reasons:

1 Much of the time spent on intelligence testing and diagnosing is wasted because it is not followed up by appropriate, related education in schools.

2 Educational psychologists are not always capable of interpreting their test results to indicate what form of treatment should be given. For instance, it is of little use to apply an intelligence test without suggesting what the result means in terms of teaching. Simply to inform a teacher that a child's I.Q. is so and so, that he has a poor memory for visual or auditory material, is suffering from mild 'brain injury' which interferes with perception and attention, or merely to supply a catalogue of item responses on the test, is of no use to most teachers. We should surely expect more assistance from educational psychologists than this. Of course, they cannot be expected to do much actual teaching. They must, however, be sufficiently experienced and knowledgeable to suggest to ordinary teachers what changes or modifications in method and approach might be made or what new techniques might be tried.

3 Many teachers are sceptical about or openly dissatisfied with the service provided at present.

When efforts to help slow readers in the Primary School's normal organization have failed, and particularly when marked failure is generalized to all basic subjects. Special Classes should be organized for them where possible. These classes should be for about fifteen children and should be taken by good, specially trained teachers. Conditions in such classes should be on a par with those in Special Schools. The segregation of such children should be as limited as possible—they should combine with other children for as many activities as they are able to profit by. If the need is too great for one Special Class to meet, and if more than one class is impossible to organize, then priority should be given to the younger children, say, the seven- and eight-year-olds.

The Primary School in its efforts to prevent backwardness in reading must organize its teaching so that it truly educates the *whole child*. An atomistic approach based on the teaching of individual subjects fitted into a rigid, time-tabled programme will not achieve the total, well-integrated, orderly development of each child. In respect of reading, for instance, the development of reading skills depends upon what happens in all lessons—physical education, art and crafts, music and number, as well as in reading or language lessons *per se*. A successful start to reading cannot be made until a certain level of psychoneurological maturity has been reached. The child must have certain visual and auditory perceptual skills, motor and psycholinguistic abilities before he becomes capable of perceiving, organizing and interpreting the symbols and sounds involved in the reading process. A total, integrated approach is therefore necessary in which the teacher uses *all* her teaching as a contribution to developmental reading.

Backwardness is perhaps as much a social problem as it is an educational one. Somehow or other the Primary School, and indeed all schools, must be involved in the sociological aspects of education. Attempts must be made to enlist parental co-operation, to change those influences in a child's background which militate against his educational progress. The size of the problem is so frightening that teachers often feel that they are impotent to do anything about it. Nevertheless, some schools make valiant attempts chiefly through such things as Open Days and Parent-Teacher Associations. More often than not, however, these fail to attract the parents of backward children.

It then becomes necessary for the school to take itself to the children's homes and parents. Some teachers of slow learners do visit the children's homes, but teachers should not be expected to become part-time social workers in addition to their professional work.

Realistic attempts to prevent backwardness must involve social workers and health visitors working as members of the school staff or, failing this, in much closer co-operation with schools than exists at present. This would almost certainly lead to the arousing and sustaining of the parents' interest in the school's work and its efforts to educate children as individuals. It is well known that backward children are often not interested in school. They come from homes where education is viewed as being of little importance and in which strong antagonisms exist towards schools and teachers. Children from such homes are thus likely to find school irksome and to have difficulty in understanding the importance of learning. They lack determination and persistence and are difficult to motivate.

Many teachers can cite examples to demonstrate the great improvements that can accrue from attempts to change parental attitudes and to obtain their co-operation. In my own school we have had surprising gains in reading attainments and personality when, as a result of the joint efforts of teachers and our social worker, parents have become enthusiastic about the school and anxious to co-operate fully with it in helping their children.

3 *Identifying the problem*

The early identification of potential reading difficulty is, of course, an important factor in prevention. It is a tragic, yet not an infrequent occurrence, to encounter children whose reading backwardness has not been dealt with by the time they reach the post-Primary stage in their education. Of course, reading difficulty will have been noted by teachers before this, but only by the child's failure to respond to teaching and his consequent lack of achievement. Prevention of reading failure, however, depends on an early identification of the *reasons* why a child is failing to respond to the school's reading programme. These reasons are never particularly easy to isolate even by a highly trained and skilled diagnostician. An attempt at suggesting a more detailed, comprehensive diagnostic programme will be made in later chapters. For the present, it is proposed to list some of the signs and conditions which may indicate to *a class teacher* that difficulty in reading is likely to arise.

In the previous chapters the importance of reading readiness was emphasized and an outline of a readiness programme was given. Were this programme incorporated in the school's scheme for encouraging developmental reading, teachers would be made more aware of individual differences and variations in speed of maturation. They would, *pari passu*, become more observant of children's responses to those activities and exercises which are designed to enhance the development of skills, abilities and attitudes prerequisite to successful reading. They would also be in a better position to make an early, although somewhat superficial diagnosis of difficulties. Following the programme, or a modified version of it, would do much to prevent failure, if our own experience is reliable.

The following suggestions are intended as a guide to teachers of younger children to help them more readily identify children to whom reading may be difficult. They might also, in some cases, be suggestive of preventive methods.

1 *Estimate the child's level of intelligence*. This cannot be done by using group intelligence tests which depend upon reading. Non-verbal or, more accurately, non-reading group tests such as the Otis Primary or Sleight Non-verbal[1] tests, may be used, but too much reliance must not be placed on any I.Q. or Mental Age arrived at for giving a definite indication of intellectual readiness for reading. Perhaps the best guide is to assess the child's language level in relation to his peers by noting the size of his spoken vocabulary, the facility with which he communicates, the length and complexity of sentences he uses, and his ability to respond to commands and

[1] Both obtainable from G. G. Harrap and Co., 182 High Holborn, London, W.C.1.

requests and to interpret stories. If test results and an assessment of language development indicate a poor intellectual level, then it is usually wiser to defer formal instruction in reading and concentrate on developing readiness, particularly in the language area.

2 *Estimate the level of the child's neurological and perceptual development.* Such an estimation will be new to most teachers. However, there is now mounting evidence that these aspects of growth are of significant importance in the acquisition of reading skills.

Of course, teachers cannot be expected to be neurologists, but they can observe signs which indicate neurological immaturity or abnormality. The following are some of the things to look for in assessing a child's readiness:

a Do his movements appear to be awkward, jerky and uncontrolled?
b Is there evidence of difficulty in eye-muscle control?
c Does he find it difficult to balance on either foot?
d Does he appear to be lacking in rhythm, e.g. in walking, marching, running, skipping, singing?
e Does he have difficulty in using a pencil or paint brush?
f Can he draw the following forms as well as the majority of his peers?

○ + □ ▭ × △ ◇ ◊ ⊠

In assessing the quality of these drawings, teachers should remember that it is the accuracy of form perception which is important. Children with motor difficulties which, for instance, interfere with the fine manipulation of a pencil point may not *draw* the figures well but their drawings may still indicate good ideas of form.

We have now studied the drawings of over a thousand children, the majority of whom were in the age range four to eight years. The remainder were older children who were experiencing considerable difficulty in learning to read. Teachers from all over the country sent drawings to the author and gave each child's chronological age and reading age on the Burt and Schonell Graded Word Tests. It appeared that, except in some older children who through practice and sophistication could draw the figures, a child was unlikely to make successful progress in reading if his form perception of any of the figures was poor. What constitutes poor form perception is at present somewhat subjective (as is the case, for instance, in the Binet-type tests where examples are given as a guide). We are working on an analysis of the drawings in an attempt to arrive at an objective assessment or scoring system. All we can claim at present is that the quality of the form perception indicated by the drawings does appear to be a very useful guide to reading readiness if a visual approach is to be used. For a child who is unable to read, if the drawings indicate good form perception then some other causes of failure should be sought; for example, the child may have auditory, emotional, or attentional difficulties, or he may have been taught by wrong methods. On the evidence of the drawings, reports have been written for teachers giving indications of readiness and/or possible reasons for reading failure. Many have written to say how very useful the reports were in helping to improve teaching either by giving more emphasis to a readiness programme or by changing the methods used.

g Does cerebral dominance appear to have been established? This is particularly important when looking at older children because dominance ought to have been established by 6–7 years. Children before this age may be more or less ambidextrous and show reversals in writing letters and words or drawing figures and shapes. They may also show rotational difficulties when copying figures and shapes—these rotations may be complete inversions such as writing 'u' for 'n' or turning figures through ninety degrees, e.g. 8 may be reproduced as ∞. Lack of cerebral dominance will also reveal itself in the child having difficulty in right-left orientation. The child is not certain of the left and right side of his body; he is unable to indicate his left hand, right ear, left foot, etc., with absolute certainty. If parts of his body are touched, he has confusion in distinguishing his own *laterality* (i.e. internalized right-left discrimination). He may also have difficulty in externalizing his laterality and is uncertain of the right-left arrangement of the space and objects around him (i.e. directionality is uncertain).

Poor laterality and directionality may be shown by a child's poor representation of his body image and concept when drawing a man. He may also have difficulty in crossing his own mid-line when drawing, e.g. when drawing a circle he may draw one half first (usually the left) and add the other half separately; he has difficulty in completing the drawing of the circle in one continuous movement. If these difficulties persist after the age of 6–7 years, reading difficulty may exist.

b In most children the left cerebral hemisphere becomes dominant (at birth the two hemispheres probably have an equal potential for dominance). This is perhaps due to the fact that those parts of the human brain concerned with language are usually found in the left hemisphere. Thus, since most of our actions are mediated by language, the left hemisphere assumes dominance because more nerve fibres are involved in it. We need not go into brain function in any greater detail here except to point out that there does appear to be a definite relationship between the development of higher language functions and the establishment of cerebral dominance. Neurological immaturity and abnormality may therefore manifest itself in poor language development, speech defects, and difficulties in language reception and expression.

Extreme forms of language difficulty may be due to aphasic conditions: receptive aphasia when the child has difficulty in decoding language symbols although the receptor organs are healthy; expressive aphasia in which the child can receive language stimuli and deal with them internally but cannot express the end result in words and/or writing although the motor aspects of expression may be intact. Such cases are fortunately rare, but mild aphasia or dysphasia may be more prevalent in young children than we imagine, at least until the psycholinguistic processes have reached maturity.

The psychoneurological aspects of reading will be dealt with more fully later, but the above list of symptoms of neurological disturbance give some indication of what class teachers may look for. They also suggest that teachers should organize activities which will help to hasten the orderly organization of the child's neurological processes. Physical education should include activities and exercises to give the child:

a a greater awareness of his own body—its structure, symmetry and balance;
b to develop laterality and directionality;
c to develop rhythmic abilities, good posture and graceful movements.

Art and Craft lessons should provide training in form appreciation and reproduction, and in visual rhythms, and give opportunities for the development of tactile abilities. In my own school, we actually train children to appreciate and accurately produce the shapes given in *2 f* above. We think that this training improves visual learning and helps the child to get meaning out of visual perception. The child draws round templates of the shapes in various sizes, he feels the shapes while they are hidden from view and classifies them. He *talks* about them, draws them freehand, and uses them in constructing pictures and patterns. (See Chapter 3 for training in Form Perception.)

As we shall see later, it may be advantageous to encourage unilateral dominance once it becomes clear that the child has begun to show a preference for one side or the other. The importance of this is still the subject of much debate and more work of an experimental nature is required before firm acceptance is possible. It is still impossible to say, for instance, whether *mixed dominance* (a lack of clear preference for one side in all activities—handedness, footedness, eyedness) or *cross-laterality* are important causes of poor reading. However, many children with severe reading disability and language difficulties do show clear evidence of mixed dominance. It might be advisable to strengthen the child's preferred side—particularly hand and foot—until unequivocal preference has been established. Once this has been done the child may later develop ambidexterity without detracting from reading progress. Training in the correction of reversals must certainly be undertaken whether the child is right- or left-handed (see Chapter 2).

3 *Make sure that the child's visual acuity and hearing are within normal limits.* If they appear to be deficient, take the necessary steps for diagnosis and treatment to be effected.

4 *Ascertain whether there is a familial incidence of reading difficulty as evidenced in the retarded development of those abilities and skills involved in learning to read.* There is no evidence that this is inherited, but congenital and other factors may be involved—complications during gestation, difficult births, abnormal parent-children relationships—predispositions towards certain illnesses such as meningitis, high fever, recurrent bronchitis and other respiratory diseases, nervous conditions, epilepsy. If the child is known to have intelligent parents and is very markedly the 'odd man out' in an otherwise normal family, suspect some pathological condition and expect emotional complications. Children whose development appears to have been influenced by these factors may be beyond the help of a teacher working in a class situation. They usually constitute severe behaviour problems in any case. However, much can be done if expectancy levels are lowered and a more intensive application of the readiness programme already outlined is used.

5 *Observe and anticipate difficulties as progress in reading is being made.* We have stressed the developmental nature of reading

and outlined the way in which we believe this development takes place in the majority of children. The results achieved in the author's school suggest strongly that the general thesis upon which the developmental reading programme is based is acceptable. There are, of course, some children who, because of variations or anomalies in growth and development, require modifications to the programme. For instance, because of the individual differences we have noted, some children may need a phonic approach more or less from the beginning. Their auditory perception seems stronger than visual, and they are therefore able to use an analytical approach much earlier. There are those who respond to a visual method very quickly and, often because they are more intelligent or strongly motivated, appear to cope with phonic analysis without the need of an organized phonic programme. Thus, several bright children using our early readers have progressed so dramatically in all aspects of reading development that at seven they have reading ages of between ten and twelve years. It is likely, perhaps, that they would have been excellent readers no matter what scheme had been used.

In identifying reading problems class teachers should therefore be watchful of each child's progress and be prepared to be diagnosing and treating any difficulties which hinder the orderly, continuing acquisition of reading skills. This does not mean that they have to use published diagnostic tests. The observant teacher can discern difficulties in the course of her teaching. She does not need tests to discover that a child suffers from reversals, directional confusions, has difficulties in blending or comprehension, reads individual words rather than phrases, and so on. These things are obvious to her. When she finds them, treatment based on the suggestions already given should follow immediately. If these fail, then she should use an appropriate remedial method from those described later in this book, if this is possible in her teaching situation. If failure persists, she should then seek expert advice and not be afraid to admit that she and the child need additional help and guidance.

Teachers may now be better aware of the many abilities

involved in learning to read and the widely differing rates at which they develop not only in different children but also within the individual child. Early identification of difficulties and variations in development is thus of very great importance in designing efforts to reduce backwardness.

PART TWO

Remedial teaching of reading

9 General remarks and principles

In the light of many years' experience with extremely retarded readers, it is claimed that the methods described in Part One, if applied systematically and appropriately (i.e. in relation to each child's development), will not only hasten reading success for 'normal' children but will also prevent failure in many cases. They have proved effective with older children who, for a variety of reasons, have previously failed to make progress. Backward readers, including brain-damaged children, coached individually or in small groups have also responded most encouragingly. Indeed, it is the *proved*[1] success of the reading scheme that makes for confidence in recommending it. Nevertheless, there have been some failures and the following chapters will concentrate on the diagnosis and remediation which have been developed as a result of the intensive investigation of failure in children. They are therefore of special importance to doctors, educational psychologists, and remedial teachers. However, they will contain much that is of interest and usefulness to all teachers, and particularly those who work with backward children.

By remedial teaching is meant teaching which is based on a

[1] See Chapter 6, p. 51, for results obtained.

differential diagnosis which forms the basis for scientific remedial procedures. We would again stress the difference between this approach and coaching, which is largely based on trial-and-error methods. The difference is made clearer if we view remedial treatment as *basic* or *central*, i.e. it deals with the underlying primary causes which have hindered the psychophysiological development of processes involved in reading; and coaching as being *peripheral* in that it treats symptoms without attempts to discover the causes of anomalous development. In a private communication,[1] Professor S. A. Kirk has described what he calls a 'scientific pedagogy' for children with learning difficulties. These disabilities he defines as a 'disorder, retardation, or delayed development in one or more of the processes of speech, language, reading, writing and other psycholinguistic disabilities caused by a possible cerebral dysfunction and/or emotional or behavioural disturbance and not the result of severe and irremediable mental retardation, sensory or cultural deprivation, or instructional factors'. The scientific pedagogy is based on the identification and differentiation of specific disabilities through longitudinal training. In a later chapter we shall describe and discuss his diagnostic instrument, the Illinois Test of Psycholinguistic Abilities, although we may wish to know more of what he means by 'severe and irremediable'. We mention his work here to give one example of the form we believe remedial education should take.

Some of the principles involved in Remedial Education of severe reading disabilities are:

1 Diagnosis and treatment should be undertaken as early as possible to avoid the development of associated emotional and behaviour disturbances which would make a differential diagnosis and treatment more difficult later on.

2 Diagnosis should include efforts to discover the level in psychoneurological development at which the child

[1] S. A. Kirk, C. Kass and B. Bateman, *The Educability of Psycholinguistic Functions in Retarded Children* (Inst. of Res. on Excep. Chn., University of Illinois: 1962).

appears to be able to function normally. This would include an assessment of the child's sensory and perceptual processes, language and motor development, intelligence and environmental adaptation. This, of course, calls for an understanding of the complexity of the child's mental development and of the psychophysiological processes involved in reading. This understanding may lead to the discovery of those links in the reading process which are deranged and those which are intact. Remediation will then be organized so that intact processes may be used to overcome or compensate for any derangement or anomaly. For example, if tactile and kinaesthetic links and abilities appear to be normal they should be used to overcome visuo-spatial or auditory difficulties.

Inability to read, sometimes called dyslexia, is a secondary disorder resulting from primary causes. The diagnosis should attempt to break down the dyslexia[1] into component elements so as to isolate the principal cause. Thus all sensory channels and their integration must be investigated; perceptual activity, which cannot in practice be isolated from sensation, must be analysed; psycholinguistic processes must be tested.

3 Remedial reading should be viewed as a means of improving communication, and language development should therefore be included in treatment. This is particularly important, for instance, in the treatment of children whose reading failure appears to centre round defective hearing and an inability to discriminate phonemes. Auditory associative processes are defective and this leads to lack of development of automatic language so that the child's speech is ungrammatical. Remedial reading will therefore have little chance of success unless the ungrammatical language is also tackled systematically and simultaneously.

4 There is no one method of dealing with reading difficulties.

[1] *The Health of the School Child, 1964 and 1965*, H.M.S.O., London, 1966, pp. 58–63.

Methods and techniques must be selected to suit the individual and be related to diagnosis.

5 A more therapeutic approach is needed. Tansley and Gulliford[1] state: 'The approach usually needs as much attention to psychological factors as to purely educational ones, but above all the teaching must inspire the non-reader to new efforts and increased confidence.' The establishment of good teacher-child relationships which encourage co-operation, hopefulness, renewed interest and enthusiasm, and a will to succeed is absolutely essential. The teacher must establish a partnership with the child in tackling what is in essence a problem for both of them. It is by no means rare to find children who have been diagnosed as hopelessly 'word blind' making excellent progress once good motivation has been created.

6 A feeling of success must be engendered from the beginning. This presupposes that the remedial team must investigate the child's reading abilities so as to establish the level in the development of reading processes at which the child is capable of functioning normally (see 1 above).

7 Diagnosis and treatment should be continuous and interdisciplinary. The amount of interdisciplinary co-operation will vary from case to case but could involve neurologists, psychiatrists, educational psychologists, audiologists, ophthalmologists, teachers, social workers, and parents. At the risk of offending some of our professional colleagues, we must emphasize however that in the final analysis the treatment is often largely an educational matter. It is the remedial teacher who eventually has to engineer success.

8 A comprehensive diagnosis must include an appraisal of how the child has reacted to his failure. Answers to the following questions must be sought:

a What is his present emotional state?
b What have been his experiences in school and at home?
c How has his personality development been affected?

[1] *The Education of Slow Learning Children.*

9 Remedial treatment should be given in the child's school wherever possible. This can help to reduce anxiety, ensure daily sessions for treatment, and encourage other teachers, who are involved in his education, to understand his problems and to work in close co-operation with the remedial team.

10 Since diagnosis may take several days and involve many professional disciplines, reading clinics should be set up. These clinics should also be responsible for research because our knowledge is still often very elementary, particularly in the treatment area.

10 Diagnostic programme

Because of the complexity of the problem it is difficult to determine exactly what information should be sought in a full diagnostic investigation, but the following is an attempt to outline a comprehensive programme. However, before proceeding with the programme details, the following suggestions must be stressed:

1 The diagnosis should reveal as clearly as possible the *primary causes* of the disability and the present levels of skills and attainments. It should give a complete picture of the child as an individual in a social setting. It should attempt to determine whether the reading disability is primary (i.e. aetiologic or developmental) or secondary (i.e. acquired or psychogenic, due to reaction to early failure, faulty instruction, contact with a family in which there is an incidence of speech defect and retarded language, or other environmental deprivations). It should therefore reveal whether the capacity to read is intact but has not developed for environmental reasons or because of environmentally conditioned states, or whether the capacity has been limited by brain injury, irreversibly low intellectual functioning, neurological disorganization, or sensory and other types of pathology.

2 The diagnosis should discover strengths as well as weaknesses.

3 The diagnostician should be sufficiently trained and experienced to differentiate between real disability or anomaly and disability which is simply due to slow maturation and underdevelopment.

4 Diagnosis should be made as early as possible not only to avoid future complications, but also in order that treatment may begin while the child's neurophysiological state is malleable, and cell associations and alternative nerve pathways are available for facilitation.

Physical examination

1 Health and physical development

The child's present physical condition should be thoroughly investigated and his previous medical history studied. Quite frequently, backward children are found to have had a history of recurrent bronchitis, suspected pulmonary tuberculosis, pneumonia, asthmatic conditions, and minor heart conditions. They are often found to be malnourished and prone to frequent catarrhal infections, stomach upsets and nervous debility. Some of these complaints may be psychosomatic in origin. There is also a rather high incidence of teeth and palate malformation which often requires orthodontic treatment if speech improvements are to be made.

Good physical health is essential for good mental health, and efficient response to stimulation and learning situations. As part of treatment, many children we have helped have needed long periods of health rehabilitation through good feeding, regular sleep, physical activity and medical treatment. About a third of our children during an average stay of four and a half years have to be seen by consultants of one sort or another. The vast majority of these children have had to be seen because of ear, nose or throat complaints.

Since we are particularly concerned with reading disability, and since, as has been pointed out earlier, reading is a psychoneurological process, *a thorough neurological examination is essential.* Children with acute reading difficulties are often found to have non-specific awkwardness in motor functioning characterized by uncoordinated, jerky, and clumsy movements, and involuntary tics, body rocking, eye-blinking, chewing and sucking. Eye-muscle difficulties are sometimes present—for instance, as seen in eye-muscle artefacts in the electroencephalogram tracings for our children. Facial and occasionally body asymmetry, anomalies in muscle tone, bilateral variations in responses to sensory stimulation, mild dysphasias and agnosias may be additional characteristics. Left-right confusions and evidence of delayed establishment of cerebral dominance are frequent. Coupled with these one finds poor ideas of body parts and structure, poor body concept and body image. For example, children are unable to name parts of their bodies, to touch named parts of the body, replicate demonstrated body positions, or assume body positions when they are described verbally.

It is, of course, necessary for the neurologist, along with other members of the diagnostic team, to distinguish between neurological abnormalities which are due to maturation lag and those due to disorganization or minimal brain damage. This is difficult because present techniques are somewhat crude. However, it ought to be possible for the neurologist to determine the levels of neurological development at which the child, irrespective of age, appears to be functioning normally. The treatment recommended by Delacato[1] and his co-workers is based on re-structuring and re-educating the child's neurological organization starting at the level of normal development the child exhibits. This form of treatment will be referred to in more detail later. The high incidence of neurological disturbance in reading-disability cases makes it important to discover and apply remedial methods to overcome or compensate for it.

[1] C. H. Delacato, *The Treatment and Prevention of Reading Problems* (Charles C. Thomas: Springfield, Ill.: 1959); and *The Diagnosis and Treatment of Speech and Reading Problems* (Charles C. Thomas: 1963).

2 Sensory development

Any necessary tests of visual and auditory acuity should be carried out and corrective measures taken. If visual and auditory difficulties persist in the absence of any discernible acuity loss or after corrective measures, then further investigations should be instituted. Remedial staffs should be aware that difficulties can arise even when the receptive organ (the eye and the ear) is healthy and functioning normally. Thus a child may have normal vision but still be perceptually 'blind' if any of the neural pathways concerned with the reception, analysis, integration, and expression of visual symbols is out of action or damaged. Similarly, a hearing child may be perceptually deaf. It is not possible to deal with these disabilities in any greater detail here but the reader is referred to Lise Gellner[1] for further information about and discussion of the neurophysiology involved.

Reading is not a visual and auditory skill alone, but involves the integration of other sensory channels to a greater or lesser degree. It is therefore important to test the functioning of kinaesthetic-movement and tactile-cutaneous sensory channels. If all sensory channels are not working and integrating normally, with good language and motor connections, then the likelihood of reading difficulty is greatly increased because the necessary processing of sensory inputs will be deficient. It may thus be necessary for children with severe disability (say, so-called 'word-blind' children) to look at each channel of sensation and to discover how it integrates with other channels. In such instances, the following diagnostic techniques should be employed:

1 Visual channels Investigate acuity, binocular vision, good fusion, good central and peripheral vision, controlled eye-movements, dominant and controlling eye (see Chapter 12 on Delacato Method).

[1] L. Gellner, *A Neurophysiological Concept of Mental Retardation and its Educational Implications* (Dr. Julian D. Levinson Research Foundation for Mentally Retarded Children: Chicago 1959).

2 *Auditory channels* Investigate auditory acuity, ability to distinguish common sounds, ability to discriminate between speech sounds and phonemes, level of automatic language, any evidence of receptive or expressive aphasia, e.g. does the child frequently give inappropriate answers to simple questions which he appears to hear?

3 *Kinaesthetic and motor channels* *When blindfolded*, can the child do the following:

a Repeat body movements demonstrated by the teacher moving parts of the child's body, e.g. if the teacher raises the child's right arm to a horizontal sideways position and then replaces it to the side, can the child repeat the movement?

b Repeat movements in space, e.g. if the teacher moves the child forward two steps and then one step to the right, can the child repeat the movements?

c Repeat the drawing of shapes, e.g. if the child holds a pencil in his hand and the teacher, holding the pencil above the child's hand, draws a simple shape, can the child draw the shape without assistance? Or again, if the teacher holds the child's hand, and makes movements in the air like, for instance, drawing a triangle, can the child repeat the process?

d Draw with the finger a shape on the child's back and ask him to draw it either on paper or with his finger in the air?

4 *Tactile-cutaneous* (*haptic*) *channels* Investigate the child's ability *when blindfolded* to do the following types of exercises:

a Differentiate between different temperatures.

b Differentiate between objects according to roughness and smoothness, hardness and softness, thickness and thinness, etc.

c Cut out of plywood or stiff card a variety of shapes, let the child feel one shape, place the shape with others and ask the child to find the one he felt.

d Using shapes or objects, ask the child to put them in groups—circles, squares, triangles, balls, beads, etc.

e Tell which finger has been touched. The teacher touches a finger, takes off the child's blindfold, and asks him which finger was touched. A variation on this is to place a matchbox between two fingers and then ask the child to point out where the box was placed. Children who fail to do this are said to have *finger agnosia*—this is a sign of neurological damage, probably involving proprioceptive cells.

f Touch a part of the child's body and ask him to show or say which part was touched. In certain cases, one finds that the ability to do this varies according to which part of the body is touched—for instance, it is usually found that the face and non-preferred hand are more sensitive to touch than areas near the spine, the preferred hand and forehead. Repeat this by touching two parts simultaneously.

Sensory channel integration

We mentioned above the four sensory modalities which are of particular importance to the development of reading. These sensory channels, of course, are seldom, if ever, used in isolation. They usually function in various combinations and are almost always associated with some form of language and motor activity. Indeed, the more closely they work together, and the more language is used to mediate them, the richer is the total sensory and perceptual experience and any resultant conceptualization. Thus, the realization that sensation, perception and concept formation are closely related is the basis of good teaching which really seeks to educate the whole child.

Attempts to discover the causes of reading failure must therefore include an investigation of sensory channel interaction and integration. It will be obvious that many combinations of sensory activity occur and that a complete diagnosis should include exercises to investigate all of them. It is important to realize that sensory channel integration will involve different levels, varying from the purely reflex level to the level involving varying degrees of cerebral activity. For the present, however, we are primarily concerned with those sensory processes and levels of integration which mediate the perceptual activities involved in the early stages of reading development. The investigation of other channels of communication will be dealt with later when tests of aphasia and psycholinguistic abilities are described and discussed. It is also important to understand that the different sensory processes mature at differing rates, and that in pathological cases some channels may be extremely weak or even completely blocked.

1 Visuo-motor integration

This is involved in all forms of copying and is important in the development of form perception. It can therefore be tested by asking the child to draw the figures given on p. 74. At lower levels it can be observed by seeing how well the child dresses himself, how he plays with his toys, how he performs in tasks involving hand-eye co-ordination similar to those mentioned in the chapter dealing with the Perceptual Training Programme. The following test is particularly useful: place nine circles on the floor in the form of a 3 × 3 square with circles about two feet apart. Give the child a copy of the floor pattern with instructions marked to indicate how he has to move from one circle to another. Thus, the child's card may be like the following:

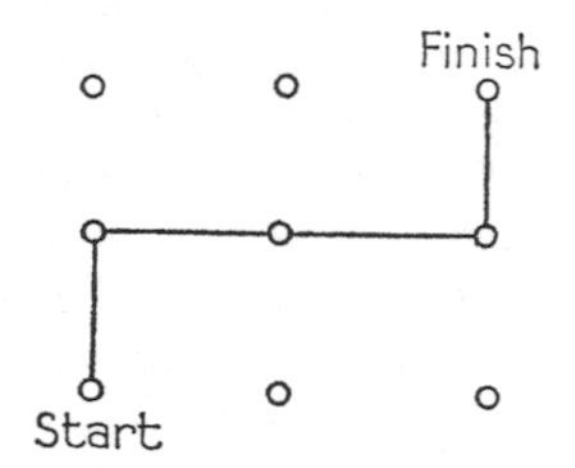

The child looks at the card and then walks the pattern indicated. The patterns increase in difficulty. If the child can walk the patterns without reference to the card, he shows good visuo-motor integration. When walking the patterns the child moves forward, sideways or backwards as required—he does not turn on any spot. When using the cards for training purposes, the child is encouraged to say forward, sideways, backward, to the right, to the left, as he moves. (Start and finish may be reversed.)

This exercise may now be reversed—help the child to walk a pattern and then ask him to select which pattern he walked.

2 *Visuo-auditory integration*

Any derangement of this will, of course, be quickly observed. However, there are a few cases in which true aphasia clearly demonstrates lack of integration of visual and auditory stimuli. For example, Margaret could repeat a number given to her verbally, but could not relate the number to its symbol. Heather could answer questions correctly in writing but could not, having read the question correctly, always give the answer orally. Colin can copy visual rhythms but cannot apply sounds to them: he can copy —— —— but is unable to connect *dah, dah* to the pattern.

In testing phonic readiness, difficulty in the visuo-auditory interaction may show itself in difficulties in associating symbols with sounds and vice versa.

3 *Visuo-kinaesthetic integration*

To test this the following exercises may be used:

1 Let the child copy a figure without being able to see what his hand is doing.

2 *Blindfold the child.* Let him hold a pencil in the normal way; hold the top of the pencil, without touching the child's hand, and draw a figure. Take off the blindfold and ask the child to select from a group of figures which one was drawn. For example, draw △ and ask the child to select from

With children ready to build up a sight vocabulary, repeat the exercise writing a word and ask the child to select from several words which one was written. For instance, hold the child's hand and write *b i g*; now ask him to select from *boy*, *by*, *big*, *ball*.

3 *Blindfold the child* and, holding his hand, draw a figure, letter or word in the air; ask him to select what was drawn.

4 Draw a figure on the child's back and ask him to select which figure was drawn. Repeat with writing words later.

4 Visuo-haptic integration

To test this, use the following exercises:

1 *Blindfold the child* and give him an object, say a toy, to explore by feeling. Remove the blindfold and ask him to select the toy from a collection of toys.

2 Repeat the above with geometric shapes and solids.

3 Repeat, at a later state, using words made by sand sprinkled on glue.

4 Repeat 1, 2 and 3 in reverse. For instance, let the child see a toy then ask him to find it from a selection when blindfolded.

5 Audio-haptic integration

Suitable exercises are:

1 Let the child explore toys, shapes, solids and objects which are hidden from view, and ask him to describe and name them, or choose one named by the teacher.

2 Blindfold the child. Make sounds and ask him to find the object from which the sound came. For example, ring a bell and see if he can find a bell by haptic exploration; make animal noises (if these can be recorded on tape so much the

better) and ask him to find the animal from a selection of animals, etc.

(These associations can be used for visuo-auditory integration tests.)

6 *Haptic-kinaesthetic integration*

To test this, the following exercises are useful:

1. *Blindfold the child*, draw a figure as described in 3, 2; now see if he can use haptic touch to find the shape from a selection.
2. Draw a shape on the child's back and again ask him to find it haptically from a selection.
3. Let the child feel a shape haptically. Now, keeping blindfold on, hold the child's hand and draw a shape; ask the child whether the shape drawn is the same as the one he felt. Repeat, but this time draw the shape on his back.

It may not be obvious why kinaesthetic and haptic channels are important in reading; they are more obviously important in writing and must be tested in cases of dysgraphia (inability to translate auditory and visual stimuli into motor, writing patterns). In reading it is haptic and kinaesthetic memory that is important because this strengthens and enriches visual perception. Haptic and kinaesthetic experience and training are also very useful in developing laterality and directionality and in improving the child's understanding that movement expressed in symbolic form becomes a means of communication. However, it is their use in remedial techniques that highlights their significance. If they are mature and strong they can be used to develop visual channels which are weak or deranged.

The above suggestions for exploring sensory channel reaction and interrelation are, of course, simplified and atomistic. In exploring his environment, in developing from an inward-to-outward, egocentric-to-social being, and in solving real-life problems, the child uses many combinations of channels in association with movement and language. However, for the purposes of a differential diagnosis of reading disability and of relating the diagnosis to treatment, the above suggestions would seem to be adequate.

We have no normative data for the types of exercises described above. Birch[1] gives some information for visual-haptic, kinaesthetic-visual and kinaesthetic-haptic integration. Our evidence suggests, however, that if a child is unable to cope efficiently with these exercises he is most likely to experience perceptual difficulty and not be ready for a successful beginning to reading and writing. We recommend therefore that a diagnosis of reading disability should include an investigation of sensory channel integration along the lines indicated. If weaknesses exist the exercises may then be used for training purposes.

Much more research into the manner by which the child receives and responds to sensory stimuli, and the development of sensory channel integration would be most useful for improving both diagnosis and treatment. Little is known about different rates of sensory maturation and the interrelation between sensory mechanisms; threshold levels and their variation in individuals need further study; the role of language is little understood. However, despite the lack of knowledge, the work done at this school appears to have led to exciting improvements in diagnosis and remedial techniques.

Examining perceptual processes

Reading is a difficult perceptual task and it is surprising how the majority of children appear to master it with such apparent ease. However, because of the perceptual skills involved any diagnosis of reading disability must include an evaluation of the child's level of perceptual development or degrees of impairment.

The child's response to a variety of stimuli is the starting-point from which consideration of perception must begin (see

[1] H. G. Birch (ed.), *Brain Damage in Children—the Biological and Social Aspects* (The Williams and Wilkins Co.: Baltimore 1964).

above); sensation and perception are causally related and interdependent, and are associated with neurological and language growth. They are also dependent upon experience, particularly in sensori-motor areas. If a child has not had rich experience in exploring his environment and his own body—for instance, as occurs in babies who are lethargic and lazy, or have been too restricted in play and general activity—perceptual development is bound to be hindered. Such a child will have been denied the opportunities to respond to a variety of stimuli and it is from the organization of such responses that perception develops. Similarly, the child whose motor development has been restricted by brain damage or whose language development has been retarded by speech difficulties, lack of stimulation, or pathological processes, will also have difficulty in perceptual tasks.

It is essential therefore to view perception in relation to the sensory-motor-language system. A disability in any of the three components of this system is likely to result in perceptual impairment or anomalous development. The importance of relating perceptual development to this system becomes even more apparent when attempts are made to direct perception in a meaningful way. For example, as far as reading is concerned, perception becomes meaningful when it is directed towards the appreciation and use of symbols as a means of communication. If these symbols were confined to pictograms the language part of the system would not be so important; however, the symbols have to be related to sounds in a highly sophisticated way if reading is to be achieved as a means of language communication. Thus, reading is not simply a perceptual-motor task (such as copying a figure, for instance); communication through reading only results when the perceptual-motor task has a verbal or conceptual element involved in and related to it.

Thus, in testing perception as it is involved in reading, consideration must be given to the following:

1 Response to sensory stimulation and sensory channel integration (already described and discussed).

2 Motor development, particularly in respect to the part it plays in perceptual processes. This again emphasizes the importance of neurological organization, right-left orientation, directionality and laterality. It also highlights the difficulty of differentiating between motor and perceptual impairment, particularly when many tests of perception involve a motor response. In assessing a child's response to a perceptual task it is important, therefore, to bear in mind the child's level of motor proficiency in relation to his age group, his general ability, language level, and response to perceptual tasks not involving an overt motor response (as in haptic appreciation, visual discrimination, closure and classification of shapes). Elaine is a girl who illustrates this. She is obviously brain-damaged, has neurological abnormalities, cannot perform motor tasks, has difficulty in crossing her mid-line, is left-handed, has finger agnosia, and at eleven years of age cannot name a circle, square or oblong. She cannot draw a man or copy shapes and has extremely poor motor co-ordination and control. However, her language development is reasonable and she is better at visual discrimination, figure and picture completion, haptic appreciation, putting pictures in temporal sequence and classification of shapes. Her perceptual-motor activity is extremely poor but one has the feeling that her perception is better than test results indicate—her motor disability is the big handicap.

3 Language development, with particular reference to those parts of speech which are involved in the structuring of perceptual-motor activities. One often has the feeling that either the child does not understand the nature of the task or that he cannot use language to help him solve a perceptual problem. Stephen was failing hopelessly on the visual-motor task described above on p. 94. He had no idea how to analyse the visual pattern and produce the motor response. It was discovered that he could not count the circles with one-to-one correspondence, he did not know the meaning of the words *forward*, *backward*, *sideways*,

across, *near*, *far*. For instance, when asked to walk forward he did not understand the instruction. Half an hour's teaching of the language involved and of relating body movement to verbal instructions, led to immediate improvement in visuo-motor activity.

This boy's difficulties emphasize an aspect of perception which is often neglected, viz., that it also involves three dimensions and a space-movement factor. The child has to project his perceptions on to his environment in order to organize and integrate it and make sense out of it. The child must therefore develop ideas of his body in relation to extra-self space. There is thus a close relationship between directional orientation, body movement and perception. In the case of Stephen, his perception in two dimensions is improving with greater control and awareness of his own movements in space. For example, by walking and running in circles his form perception of circles has improved.

Perception also involves attention, concentration, memory, retention and recall. Many children with reading difficulties are atypical children. One characteristic which occurs frequently is lack of attention which results from restlessness and distractibility, rigidity, over-involvement, or acute withdrawal from learning situations. Their performance on perceptual tasks therefore varies. Jane is an epileptic girl who has frequent *petit mal* episodes. She is extremely difficult to teach and her varying performance in the perceptual training programme is exasperating. On the few occasions when her attention can be held she responds encouragingly. At other times, she gives the impression of being quite ineducable. If a way could be found to stabilize her attention it would be quite possible to teach her to read.

Another characteristic is inadequate memory span. Children with reading difficulties tend to have a weakness in visual and auditory memory. They not only have deficient inventories of visual and auditory images, but are also weak in remembering sequential arrangements of visual and auditory images. Many children in our school population have, for example, unusually low scores on the visual and auditory sequencing sub-tests on the *Illinois Test of Psycholinguistic Abilities* (I.T.P.A.). This poor memory span affects their perceptual development and is a pronounced handicap in learning to read, because reading is predominantly a matter of building up a store of immediately recognizable visual and auditory images and sequences.

In previous chapters hearing and auditory perception have been mentioned and discussed and there is little else to be added. A diagnosis of perception, however, must include tests of auditory perception and an examination of any apparent failure to interpret what is heard. Perceptual deafness might have to be investigated; this is dealt with more fully in the next two sections.

Tests of perception

A great deal of research into perceptual processes has been carried out but results are often inconclusive; much of the research has been related to perceptual processes which do not appear to be directly involved in reading and which do not, in any case, permit the use of accessible, easily applied tests. The majority of the following tests are generally well known, easily obtainable and quickly administered. They are, however, chiefly perceptual-motor tasks and it is necessary therefore to reiterate the caution that from inadequacy in these tasks it is not always possible to infer perceptual disturbance. Nevertheless, an experienced examiner should be able to differentiate between inadequacies caused by motor defects or inadequate motor experiences and development, and those due to perceptual difficulty. This is made easier if an examination of sensory inputs and integration has preceded the testing of perceptual processes, and if difficulties occur in tasks dealing with visual and auditory discrimination and problems of rotation and reversal.

1 Perceptual training tasks used for diagnosis

Our own diagnostic programme is based largely on the training exercises described and illustrated in the chapter dealing with our *Perceptual Training Programme*. The tasks are used as tests and the child's responses in each of the fifteen areas of training are rated on a 5-point rating scale.[1] A rating of 0 is given when the child completes the set of exercises without any difficulty; a rating of 4 is given when the child finds even the simplest in the set beyond him. The fifteen ratings give us a rough differential diagnosis of the child's perceptual abilities and indicate the areas in which systematic training appears to be necessary.

Summating the rating scores, a child with no perceptual difficulties would score 0 and a child with acute perceptual disturbance in all areas would score 60. From our results so far, a total rating score of 10+ appears to indicate possible neurological abnormality and reading difficulty. These results were obtained from 50 of our children, age range 8–15 years. When the ratings of 15 children diagnosed by our neurologist as possibly brain-damaged were compared with the ratings for 15 children who were neurologically normal, the difference between the mean total ratings for the two groups was highly significant ($P < 0{\cdot}001$).

It would, of course, be unwise to draw conclusions from this evidence—much more normative data are required from a bigger and more representative sample. However, as far as diagnosing reading readiness and perceptual disturbance sufficient to interfere with reading progress are concerned, our results do appear to be of great significance. More results are being collected particularly from random samples of four- to eight-year-olds and from older children who are experiencing reading difficulty. An analysis of these results, together with normative data, will be published later.

The perceptual tasks in our programme which appear to be of particular significance in relation to reading failure are kinaesthetic-visual and kinaesthetic-haptic integration, classification of shapes, form perception, visual discrimination, visual retention, visual copying, auditory sequencing and rhythm and hand-eye co-ordination. Ratings on closure, naming of shapes, temporal sequencing and visual sequencing

[1] See Appendix I.

do not, on the evidence accumulated so far, appear to differentiate with certainty between reading failures and successes. The exercises in closure are probably too simple for most of our children; even children who have made a successful start to reading may have difficulty in temporal and visual sequencing as we test these.

2 *Test of form perception*

We use the drawings of the standard figures given in Chapter 8, p. 74, as a test of the level of form perception required for successful reading to be achieved. Drawings have been collected from many schools, and particularly from four- to eight-year-olds. From the child's ability to recognize and reproduce these forms, extremely accurate predictions have been made of the child's readiness for reading or his reading level at a given chronological age. For the few cases where predictions have not been highly correlated with results, there has invariably been some evidence of other factors detracting from the predictive value of the drawings. These factors include the effect of minimal brain injury and poor environmental stimulation and motivation, or the use of teaching methods which emphasize the auditory rather than the visual aspects of early reading. The examples on pages 105–6 will perhaps serve to illustrate the predictive use of the drawings.

The results have not yet been standardized; nevertheless, a child who does not reproduce the first six forms reasonably accurately is not likely to make an easy, successful start to reading.

3 *Drawing-a-man test*

This test devised by Goodenough[1] in the 1920's, and later revised, is normally used for assessing intellectual levels. For

[1] F. L. Goodenough, *Measurement of Intelligence by Drawings* (World Book Co.: Yonkers, New York 1926). Available from the National Foundation for Educational Research in England and Wales, The Mere, Upton Park, Slough, Bucks.

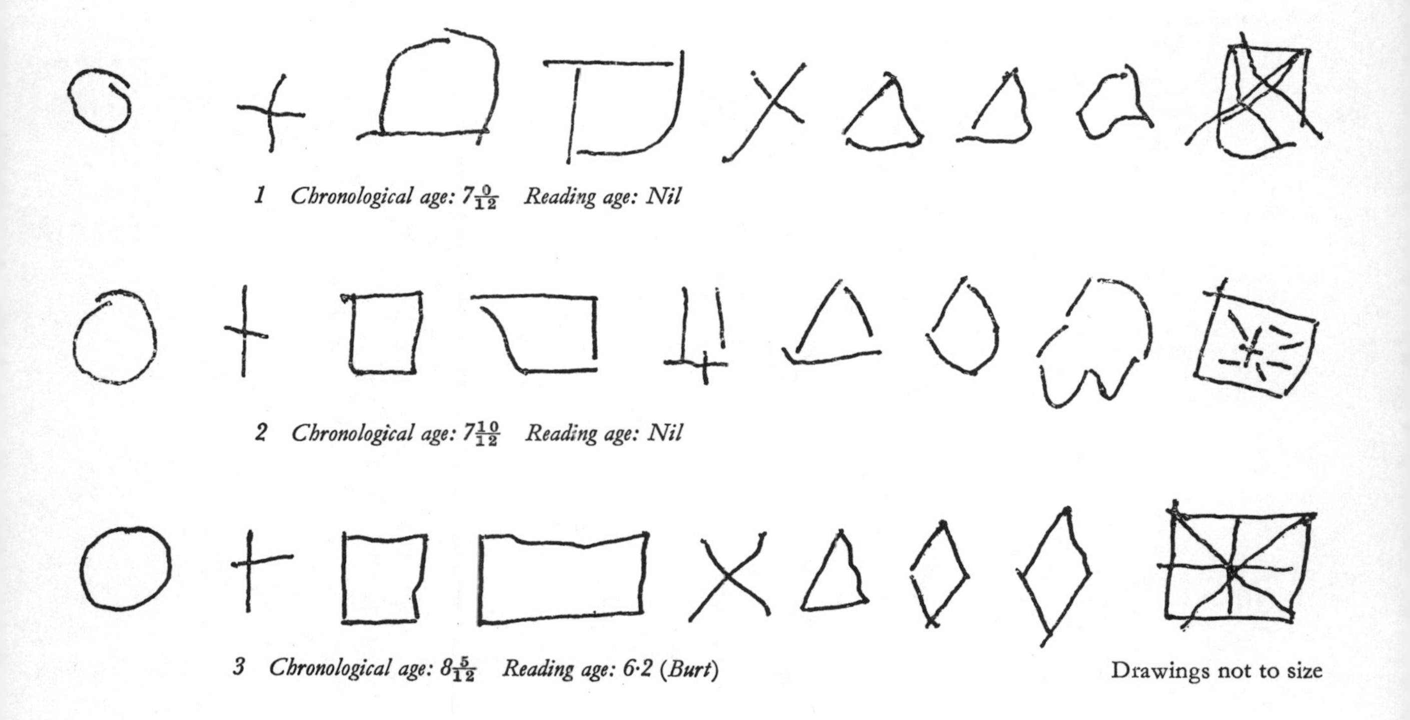

1 *Chronological age:* $7\frac{0}{12}$ *Reading age: Nil*

2 *Chronological age:* $7\frac{10}{12}$ *Reading age: Nil*

3 *Chronological age:* $8\frac{5}{12}$ *Reading age: 6·2 (Burt)*

Drawings not to size

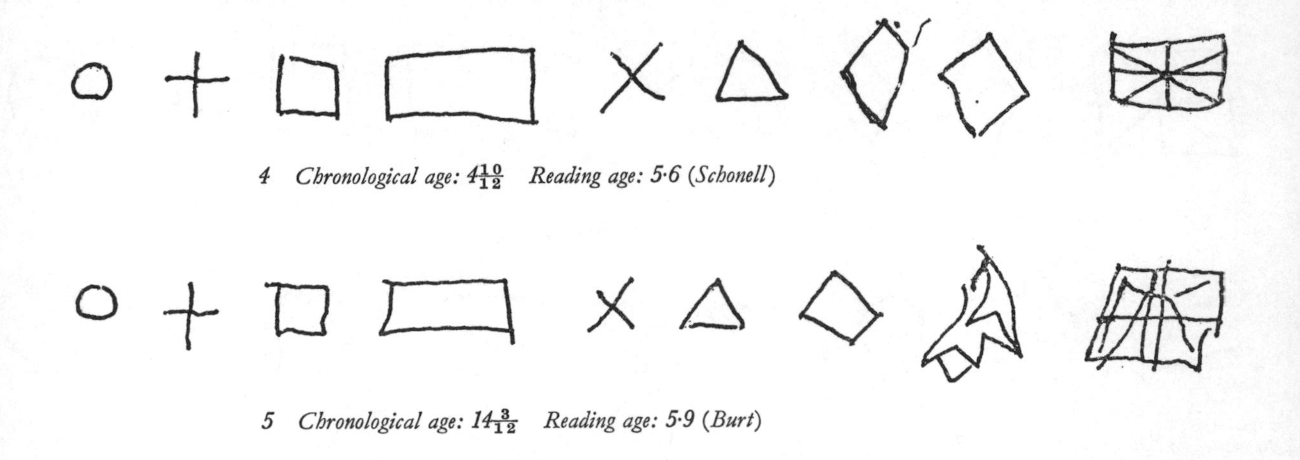

4 *Chronological age:* $4\frac{10}{12}$ *Reading age:* 5·6 (*Schonell*)

5 *Chronological age:* $14\frac{3}{12}$ *Reading age:* 5·9 (*Burt*)

6 *Chronological age:* $5\frac{5}{12}$ *Reading age:* *Nil*

Drawings not to size

our purposes, however, it is used to assess the child's perception of his body image, which has of course developed out of neurological organization, sensation, perception and experience. Children with motor difficulties, perceptual disturbance, and minimal brain injury, usually produce drawings which reflect their difficulties. A diagnosis of perceptual disability from the drawing of a man has to be related to maturational factors. Provided the interpreter has knowledge of the types of drawings produced by children of different ages and abilities, he can discover features which may indicate perceptual-motor difficulties. The following features may be significant:

1 The essential proportions of the figure and its parts.
2 The degree of integration and organization shown in the figure.
3 The degree of symmetry in relation to the mid-line.
4 The omission of body parts.
5 The angle at which the drawing stands in relation to the vertical.
6 The size and positioning of the drawing.

The drawings on pages 108–9 are examples of the drawings of children who are thought to have minimal brain injury and/or perceptual difficulties.

4 *The Bender visual motor gestalt test*[1]

This well-known test is invariably used in the examination of perceptual processes and visual motor development. It is particularly useful as an indicator of developmental disturbances caused by different types of psychopathology, e.g. brain

[1] L. Bender, *A Visual Motor Gestalt Test and its Clinical Use*, Research Monograph no. 3 (The American Orthopsychiatric Association: New York 1938). Available from the National Foundation for Educational Research in England and Wales.

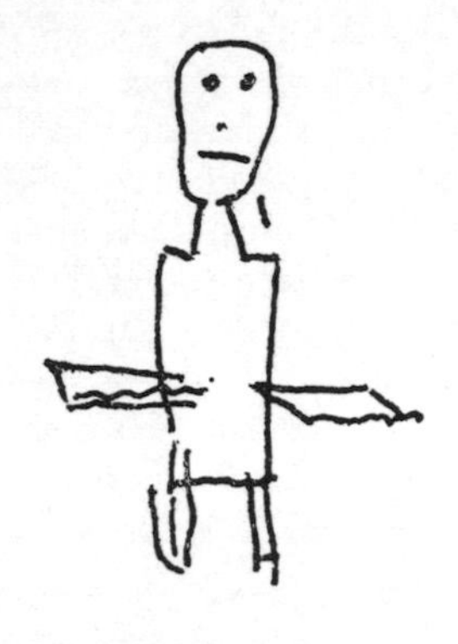

C.A. $11\frac{1}{12}$ *years*

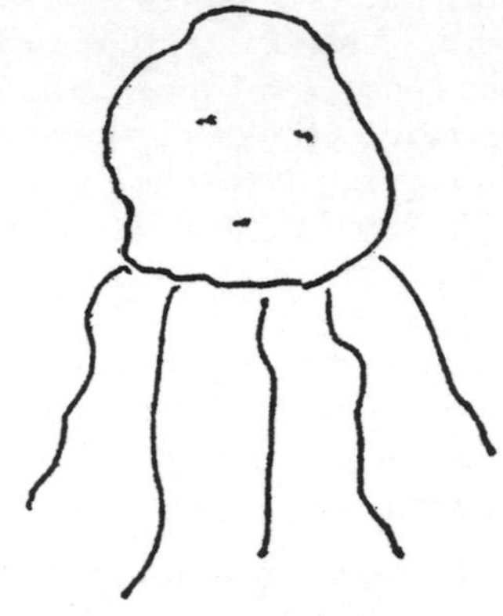

C.A. $12\frac{5}{12}$ *years*

C.A. 11 years

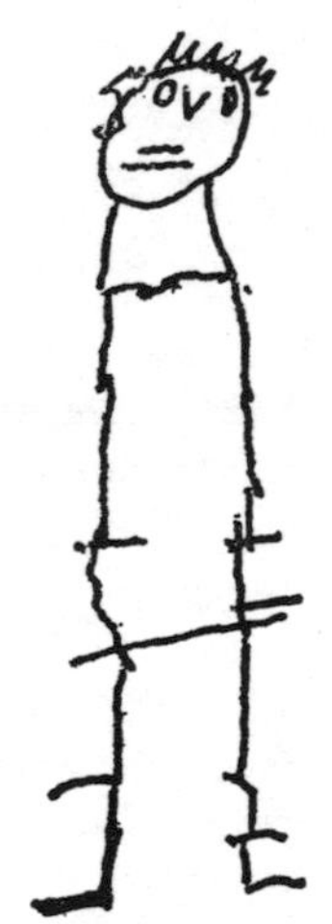

C.A. $11\frac{7}{12}$ *years*

Drawings not to size

C.A. $9\frac{7}{12}$ *years*

C.A. $10\frac{9}{12}$ *years*

C.A. $11\frac{4}{12}$ *years*

Drawings not to size

damage, psychosis, neurosis, mental retardation, and aphasic conditions.

The test is easy to administer but more difficult to score and interpret. The child is shown nine figures (gestalt forms) separately and is asked to copy them. The test has been standardized on eight hundred children aged three to eleven inclusive. All the figures should normally be satisfactorily produced at the age of eleven years. Bender claims that this test of visual-motor-gestalt function is associated with language ability, visual perception, manual motor ability, memory, temporal and spatial concepts, and organization or representation. It is therefore valuable as a guide to maturation in 'visual motor gestalt function between the ages of four and eleven—which is the age when *reading and writing are developing*' (author's italics).

In using the test as diagnostic of reading disability the following factors are important:

1 The quality, size and accuracy of the child's reproductions as compared to those of his chronological age group; size variation in the figures.

2 Evidence of rotating or reversing the drawings; difficulty with angles.

3 Evidence of perseveration in one figure or between one figure and the next presented.

4 The orientation of the figures on the paper.

5 The method of attack employed, e.g. does the child do his drawings atomistically without an apparent awareness of the gestalt? Does he use counting in copy figures composed of dot patterns? Does he work from left-to-right, right-to-left, top-to-bottom, or bottom-to-top?

5 The Benton visual retention test

Benton[1] claims that his test is 'a clinical and research instru-

[1] A. L. Benton, *The Revised Visual Retention Test. Clinical and Experimental Applications* (The State University of Iowa: 1955). Available from the National Foundation for Educational Research in England and Wales.

ment to assess memory, perception and visuo-motor functions'. There are three equivalent forms of the test, each with ten designs; the designs consist of one or more figures. The test may be administered in four different ways; for our purpose, we have used the method (Administration A) of exposing the design for ten seconds immediately followed by the child's attempt at reproduction. The test is only useful for older children (8+ years). Norms for the number of designs correctly reproduced and for total number of errors are given. Suggestions are given as to what degree of deviation from the norms is indicative of specific disability in visual memory or visuo-motor function.

Scoring the test is somewhat complicated and is based on the following aspects of reproduction: number of correct reproductions, omissions and additions, distortions, perseverations, rotations, misplacements, and size errors. The test is said to be a useful instrument in the diagnosis of cerebral injury or disease. Our own research has shown a statistically significant relationship between total error score and evidence of neurological abnormality. Older children who have severe reading disability, particularly of a visual type, are likely to have high error scores on this test. For this reason, the test is included in the diagnostic programme.

6 *Koh's Block Design*

If the Wechsler Intelligence Scale for Children is used as a measure of intellectual functioning, the Block Design Sub-Test may afford information about perceptual disturbance. This is a test of ability to analyse and synthesize perceptual information and involves visuo-motor and visuo-spatial activity. If the child has difficulty in completing the designs in an insightful way, in correctly rotating the blocks or completing the gestalt, then there must be a suggestion of perceptual disturbance. This is particularly significant if the Block Design sub-test score is markedly lower than the majority of other sub-test scores.

7 *Tests of auditory perception*

We have previously mentioned ways of detecting losses in auditory acuity or defects in auditory rhythm and sequencing. However, there are some children who suffer from 'perceptual deafness'. They have no apparent hearing loss yet still have difficulty in dealing with auditory material. Lise Gellner postulates two groups of children who have this difficulty, viz., Auditory-Somatic Group and Auditory-Autonomic Group. The former group are mute or have severe speech defects. They have difficulty in appreciating word-sound patterns, repeating heard words, and responding to commands; they often have poor number concepts because of poor memory. The latter group get little meaning from language and usually have parrot-like memories for sounds and words. They repeat words, phrases and sentences, have difficulty in speaking spontaneously, in 'finding' words and answering questions. They appear to be disinterested in stories and conversation and fail to respond to verbal requests. Both groups are sometimes classed as aphasic or dysphasic. They may have no disability in visuo-motor and visuo-spatial perception and build up sight vocabularies and learn to write quite normally. Difficulties arise when phonic analysis becomes necessary. They will be referred to again below, when tests of aphasia are mentioned. It is important to realize that these children are often difficult to manage. They are easily frustrated, appear to be aloof because they are afraid of verbal situations, can be wrongly described as lazy and negativistic, and are often underestimated intellectually. On the Wechsler Intelligence Scale for Children they are likely to have a significant performance bias. Heather, whom we have mentioned previously, appears to belong to the auditory-autonomic group; she has excellent artistic ability, made a satisfactory visual start to reading, has a performance bias in terms of I.Q. of 62 points. However, she has difficulty in answering questions, of putting words to objects and situations, of interpreting stories and dealing with number concepts. She likes music and dances gracefully but without rhythm. She has a history of problem behaviour at home and in school but, with help to adjust to her difficulty, she is much improved and is making excellent progress in language development.

8 *Tests of lateral dominance*

Since children with perceptual difficulties often appear to have failed to establish complete right or left dominance, it is deemed appropriate to include these tests in the consideration of perceptual development. If the Delacato Method of remedial treatment is to be used, these tests will be an essential part of the diagnostic programme. The tests we use are those designed by Harris.[1] Harris claims that his tests are sensitive indicators of 'directional confusion' whether or not this is closely related to crossed dominance (dominant hand and dominant eye are contra-lateral). There can be little doubt that directional confusion is significantly related to reading and spelling disability which involves reversals. It is also present in some children who have speech defects such as stuttering and lack of speech rhythms. The test consists of eleven sub-tests to determine the following:

1 Knowledge of right and left.

2 Hand dominance.

3 Eye dominance.

4 Foot dominance.

Our experience with the test tends to confirm that with our severe reading-disability cases uncertain knowledge of right and left and lack of clear hand dominance are frequently occurring characteristics. This is particularly apparent in children who have neurological abnormalities or who appear to be neurologically immature. The importance of mixed hand-eye dominance as a significant cause of reading disability is not yet

[1] A. J. Harris, *Harris Tests of Lateral Dominance*, 3rd ed. (The Psychiatric Corporation: New York 1958). Available from National Foundation for Educational Research in England and Wales.

clearly established. It is often present in poor readers but it is also often found with good readers. It may be, of course, that the good readers have managed to compensate satisfactorily; if this is the case, then mixed hand–eye dominance may be of greater significance as a cause of reading failure. Delacato is of the opinion that *complete unilateral dominance* should be established before other remedial measures are taken.

Tests of aphasia and psycholinguistic abilities

The diagnostic programme should include tests of language ability, function and development. Children with reading disability often have language or psycholinguistic difficulties of one sort or another, and in recent years a good deal of attention has been paid to the diagnosis of these difficulties and to the greater understanding of linguistic processes and the part they play in mental and social development.

1 *Examining for aphasic conditions*

Severe linguistic disturbance may be associated with varying degrees of aphasia and when it appears that the child has difficulty in receiving language stimuli or in expressing himself freely, tests of aphasia should be used. The most comprehensive of these are those devised by Jon Eisenson.[1] In the manual for these tests, Eisenson describes aphasia as including 'disabilities of some degree, in the formulation or in the expression, in the comprehension or in the production, of meaningful symbols'. He states that the following forms of associational difficulties are found:

1 The comprehension of and appropriate response to audible symbols.

2 The comprehension of visual symbols.

3 The evocation of appropriate spoken words in meaningful situations.

[1] Jon Eisenson, *Examining for Aphasia* (The Psych. Corp.: New York 1954).

4 The production of appropriate written language in meaningful situations.

These four difficulties are mentioned here to serve as guide lines to the diagnostician as to when an examination for aphasia is indicated. The manual is a most valuable document because it contains numerous tests which, when used selectively, may result in a better differential diagnosis of aphasia, dysphasia and cerebral dysfunction.

2 *The Illinois Test of psycholinguistic abilities*

This test, devised by McCarthy and Kirk,[1] is still in the experimental stage but it represents a new approach to the evaluation of language processes. It is based on the learning model of Osgood[2] and its rationale assumes that its nine sub-tests measure implicit processes in the child's language development. The approach used is necessarily somewhat atomistic, and the discreteness and validity of the sub-tests is much in doubt. Nevertheless, the test is useful, even in its present form, because it affords a means of differentiating and perhaps identifying specific disability in language function and also gives some indication of the form individual treatment should take. The test battery has been standardized on 700 children aged 2½ years to 9 years but it can be useful with older children who because of impaired intellectual development, speech and language difficulties, or deprived linguistic backgrounds are experiencing language and/or reading difficulties. Although norms giving language ages on the whole battery and for each subtest are supplied, the principal use of the battery is to afford a means of investigating abnormalities and deficiencies in individual cases. Indeed, in evaluating the usefulness of the test McCarthy and Kirk have used the Case Study approach rather than an experimental/control group approach with

[1] J. J. McCarthy and S. A. Kirk, *Illinois Test of Psycholinguistic Abilities*. Experimental Edition (University of Illinois: 1961).
[2] C. E. Osgood, *Contemporary Approaches to Cognition* (Harvard University Press: Cambridge, Mass. 1957).

representative samples. This means they have assessed a child's psycholinguistic abilities on the test, developed remedial measures related to the test findings, given individual tutoring, and then made a reassessment to determine the effects of the remediation. There may be research objections to this approach, particularly from statisticians; nevertheless, it is an approach likely to benefit children more speedily and effectively:

The design of the test is based on the rationale that three major dimensions are needed to describe a psycholinguistic ability, viz., *level* of organization, psycholinguistic or communication *process*, and *channel* of communication involved. The authors postulate two levels of organization, viz., representational and automatic sequential; three psycholinguistic processes, viz., decoding, encoding and association; only two channels are explored, viz., auditory-vocal and visual-motor. The nine sub-tests are as follows:

TEST 1 *Auditory decoding*. This consists of a series of questions to be answered by *Yes* or *No*, e.g., Do aeroplanes fly? Do barometers congratulate?

TEST 2 *Visual decoding*. This consists of a series of items to test the child's ability to select from four pictures one which is 'perceptually identical' to a previously shown stimulus picture. The stimulus picture and the selected one are not physically identical but are semantically identified. Indeed, the test is obviously testing simple classification ability in addition to visual decoding *per se*.

TEST 3 *Auditory-vocal association* is a test of analogical thinking and use of opposites, e.g. a bird flies in the air, a fish swims in the ——; iron is heavy, feathers are ——.

TEST 4 *Visual-motor association*. The child is shown a stimulus picture and then selects from four pictures one which 'goes with' the stimulus, e.g. sock goes with shoe; hammer goes with nail.

TEST 5 *Vocal encoding.* The child is shown several objects individually and is asked to 'Tell me about this.' The scores represent the number of discrete concepts enumerated and there is no theoretical limit to them.

TEST 6 *Motor encoding.* The child is shown a number of objects separately and asked to 'Show me what you should do with this.' He is then shown pictures instead of objects. All information must be in the form of gesture; no vocal response is accepted.

TEST 7 *Auditory-vocal automatic ability.* This is a test of those aspects of language usage which are so common as to be automatic. It is a grammar test to test the use of plurals, past and present participles, inflexions, and comparatives and superlatives. For example, using pictures, the examiner says, 'Here is an apple; here are two ——'; 'This man is going to wreck his car; now the car is ——', etc.

TEST 8 *Auditory-vocal sequencing ability.* This is tested by a digit-span test. The digits are presented at a rate of two a second and the child is allowed two attempts.

TEST 9. *Visual-motor sequencing ability.* The child has to duplicate a series of pictures or geometric shapes exposed for five seconds. The sequences range from two pictures to six figures.

From the scores obtained a psycholinguistic profile is constructed, using either language age norms or standard score norms. The profile is a ready guide to the child's psycholinguistic strengths and weaknesses as assessed by the test battery, and may indicate those areas where remedial action is needed. We have more than a hundred profiles of children who are of below-average intelligence, some of whom are maladjusted, brain-injured or psychotic. Some of the children are reading successfully, but the majority have acute reading disability. The following observations about the test may be useful.

1 The test certainly encourages a more scientific and systematic approach to the diagnosis of reading disability.

2 In our setting, where children are under regular observation, the test reveals little new but results generally confirm what is known or suspected.

3 Our reading failures are usually poor on visual-motor and auditory-vocal sequencing tests. Unfortunately, so are some of our reading successes. However, it appears that reading success is not likely until a language age of 6–7+ years has been reached on the two tests involved.

4 The observation above confirms that poor memory for visual and/or auditory material is often a characteristic of poor readers.

5 A 'spiky' profile is characteristic of children with sensory losses, motor disabilities, aphasic or dysphasic conditions. For example, children with slight hearing loss show deficiencies in auditory decoding, auditory-vocal automatic ability; children with visual handicaps have low scores in visual decoding and particularly in visual-motor association and visual-motor sequencing; 'brain-damaged' children usually have irregular profiles particularly if motor development is seriously affected.

6 When motivational problems are suspected as being significant in reading failure, the I.T.P.A. test often can confirm the suspicion if the profile shows no marked deficiency in any process or channel of communication.

7 Some tests in their present form do not appear to be very useful or reliable. This is particularly true for Test 1 in which test/re-test scores are often markedly different mainly, it would seem, because of the 50/50 chance of success or failure, perseveration tendencies, and lack of seriousness when harder items are used.

8 Some of the pictorial material needs to be anglicized for British children. There are also some ambiguities in the material and it has not always been selected to be related

closely to the environment of children, e.g. the motor encoding test uses far too many pictures of musical instruments to make it more a test of musical experience than of motor encoding.

9 The material used in the sub-tests indicates the type of material which might be used in remedial work.

10 The test is of considerable value in a clinical setting because it provides information from which the psychologist or remedial teacher can formulate a programme of remedial work. In the later chapters on treatment an attempt will be made to suggest types of exercise and activity which might be used to overcome specific disabilities indicated by the test profile.

The I.T.P.A. test has been described more fully than other tests because it is not yet well known and also because it represents a new approach to the diagnosis of psycholinguistic disabilities. Many of the sub-tests are not original in concept, but the manner in which they are organized round a particular learning model is an interesting development of the earlier work of Sievers,[1] who postulated the same three *processes* in language, viz., decoding, association and encoding, the two *channels* of transmission, viz., perceptuomotor and auditory-vocal but three *levels* of organization, viz., semantic, grammatical and integrational.

Tests of intelligence, language development, and educational status

1 *Tests of intelligence*

It is customary to include tests of intelligence in any diagnostic programme. The usual reasons given for this are based on the following assumptions:

[1] D. J. Sievers and C. M. Rosenburg, 'The Differential Language Facility Test and E.E.G.'s of Brain-Injured Retarded Children', *Am. J. Ment. Def.*, vol. 65, 1960, pp. 46–50.

1 The mental age arrived at will give some evidence of intellectual readiness for beginning to read. In the past, it has been generally assumed that a mental age of 6–7 years is necessary before a successful start to reading can be made.

2 The mental age will serve to differentiate between true backwardness (due to intellectual deficiency) and under-functioning or retardation (backwardness due to factors other than poor intellect).

3 The I.Q. will indicate the speed of reading development likely to be achieved, i.e. it is a predictor of future development.

There is now sufficient evidence from research and clinical experience to indicate that none of these assumptions is fundamentally acceptable in general. They are even less acceptable in most cases of acute reading disability. Teachers who are experienced in helping poor readers know that the mental age cannot be taken as a reliable guide to reading readiness. Many children who cannot read have mental ages above a 7-year level; some children who start to read successfully have mental ages below this level. These teachers also know that the concept of under-functioning, as related to mental age, is not substantiated in teaching practice. Research appears to show, and experience supports the evidence, that in a group of children with equivalent mental ages there are almost as many who over-function as under-function. It is also now accepted that the mental age should not be considered without relation to chronological or biological age; there are obvious intellectual differences between young normal and older subnormal children of the same mental age or *test age*. Indeed, our comprehensive research[1] reveals that, even in

[1] A research programme carried out by an *ad hoc* research team comprising a neurosurgeon, two consultant psychiatrists, educational psychologist, teachers, mature university students, child-care staff and a social worker. We have collected a mass of information about the physical, psychological, educational, and social development of 165 children. Computer results are to hand and various reports are being written. See A. E.

intellectual status alone, every child is unique. From what has been said previously it will be clear that so many factors are involved in reading disability that any prediction based on an I.Q. must be viewed with reserve. Perhaps we have now reached a stage in educational advance when the concept of fixed intelligence should be abandoned, and the validity and reliability of I.Q. tests in their present form should be re-examined.

We do not suggest, therefore, that an intelligence test need necessarily be included in a diagnostic programme. However, at present we do use the *Wechsler Intelligence Scale for Children*[1] as part of our attempts at a differential diagnosis. The actual verbal, performance, and full I.Q.'s are not of particular importance; we are more interested in the child's total performance, qualitatively as well as quantitatively (see Chapter 8). The following aspects of the test performance seem to be significant:

1 The difference between Verbal and Performance scores, particularly if the difference is marked—say 15 points or more; a big verbal bias may be indicative of minimal brain injury and perceptual disturbance.

2 The pattern of responses to the various sub-tests. With children who are failing in reading one frequently finds a wide scatter of responses to the sub-tests both within the two scales and on the test as a whole. Thus, for an individual child it is possible to find a range of response from above normal on some sub-tests to subnormal on others. Such a range is of obvious diagnostic importance.

The following scaled scores are taken from actual W.I.S.C. records of children who were failing in reading:

[1] D. Wechsler, *Wechsler Intelligence Scale for Children* (The Psych. Corp.: New York 1949).

Tansley, *Research into the Differential Diagnosis of Educational Subnormality, Conference Report*, 27th Biennial Conference. Assoc. for Special Education, 1964.

TEST			CHILD					
			A	B	C	D	E	F
Verbal	Information	1	4	7	3	8	8	5
	Comprehension	2	5	10	5	3	13	8
	Arithmetic	3	4	4	7	4	6	5
	Similarities	4	6	13	4	2	11	9
	Vocabulary	5	8	10	5	6	8	10
Performance	Picture Completion	6	12	16	11	13	5	6
	Picture Arrangement	7	5	6	5	5	5	6
	Block Design	8	6	11	11	10	5	6
	Object Assembly	9	8	12	10	15	4	0
	Coding	10	2	4	6	1	8	6

The responses to the various sub-tests may indicate individual difficulties or impairments and/or lack of environmental opportunity and experience. For instance, a young child who has not been allowed to play with constructional and manipulative toys is likely to do badly on tests such as block design and object assembly; a child who has been deprived of language stimulation or whose general knowledge is reduced through lack of social contacts, cultural deprivation or reading failure may have low scores on information, comprehension, similarities, picture completion and picture arrangement items; a child whose work habits are unsatisfactory may do badly on coding and picture arrangement. The pattern of test responses is thus a possible guide to how far the child has acquired the techniques of learning, rather than an assessment of his actual ability to learn. The pattern can therefore indicate those areas of intellectual activity in which remedial action is required.

3 The child's attempts at the block design and object assembly tests may indicate perceptual-motor difficulties and indicate the need for perceptual training.

4 The quality of the child's responses can indicate to what extent he is capable of benefiting from experience, of making abstractions and generalizations. Thus two children may have the same score on a sub-test but one may use trial-and-error methods plus speed and the other show real ability to analyse and synthesize in an insightful way.

5 The good examiner will note the child's reaction to success or failure, to praise and encouragement; his level of motivation and aspiration; and his relationship to the examiner. The child's responses and general reaction to the test situation therefore give some indication of his personality.

6 The correlation between the three I.Q.'s obtained and success in mechanical reading is not very high; our results for 129 E.S.N./Maladjusted children were as follows:

CORRELATION TABLE (N = 129)

	Schonell Graded Word	*Neale Speed*	*Neale Accuracy*	*Neale Comprehension*
W.I.S.C. Verbal I.Q.	0·358	0·074	0·314	0·562
W.I.S.C. Performance I.Q.	0·275	0·071	0·222	0·401
W.I.S.C. Full I.Q.	0·207	0·084	0·290	0·514

Mean W.I.S.C. Verbal I.Q. = 71
Mean W.I.S.C. Performance I.Q. = 72
Mean W.I.S.C. Full I.Q. = 69

A child's W.I.S.C. I.Q. must not therefore be regarded as too reliable a pointer to reading success or likely failure.

We have also used the *Raven Progressive Matrices (1938 and 1947)*[1] and have found them useful as an alternative to the W.I.S.C. When used in conjunction with a vocabulary scale they seem to give results which are as reliable as the W.I.S.C. results. They do not, of course, supply as much over-all information about a child's intellectual functioning and efficiency in a wide variety of test situations.

2 *Tests of language development*

In previous chapters the importance of language and assessments of language development have been stressed. The Crichton Vocabulary Scale[2] is recommended for use with

[1] J. C. Raven, *Progressive Matrices* (H. K. Lewis and Co.: London 1947).
[2] J. C. Raven, *The Crichton Vocabulary Scale* (H. K. Lewis and Co.: London 1950).

the Progressive Matrices (1947). A later vocabulary test, the English Picture Vocabulary Test, a revision by Brimer[1] of the Peabody Picture Vocabulary Test, is perhaps a better test to use.

Other tests of various aspects of language development, such as those devised by Watts,[2] may be used in particular cases. Some of the Watts tests are especially useful for younger children.

3 *Tests of educational status*

Since we are primarily concerned with reading disability we need only use tests of various aspects of reading ability. For reading accuracy, the Schonell[3] and Burt[4] tests are well known; for comprehension, the Schonell Silent reading tests may be used. The Watts Holborn Scale[5] may be used for assessing both accuracy and comprehension. However, the best test for a comprehensive evaluation of reading development is the Neale Analysis of Reading Ability.[6] This gives scores for reading accuracy, speed and comprehension and also gives diagnostic information.

The test consists of three equivalent sets of six passages of prose, each set 'forming a continuous reading scale for children aged from 6 to 12 years'. Each passage is illustrated by a picture. In addition, there are three Supplementary Diagnostic Tests. The Record Form for the test includes sections for the recording of types of error made. These errors are classified as mispronunciations, substitutions, refusals, additions, omis-

[1] M. A. Brimer and L. M. Dunn, *The English Picture Vocabulary Test*, 1962. (Distributed by the National Foundation for Educational Research.)
[2] A. F. Watts, *The Language and Mental Development of Children* (G. G. Harrap and Co.: London 1944).
[3] F. J. Schonell, *Graded Word Reading Test* (Oliver and Boyd: Edinburgh 1950).
[4] C. Burt, *A Handbook of Tests for Use in Schools*, 2nd ed. (Staples: London 1947).
[5] A. F. Watts, op. cit.
[6] M. D. Neale, *Neale Analysis of Reading Ability* (Macmillan: London 1958).

sions and reversals. The norms for the test range from 6 years to 13 years but it is suitable for older children with reading disability.

The Standard Reading Tests of Daniels and Diack[1] should be mentioned. This is a battery of tests which the authors claim 'has been designed to be given to every child who, it is evident, has not fully mastered all the skills involved in reading'. The battery consists of both attainment and diagnostic tests. Unfortunately, the attainment tests are based on degrees of phonic complexity and the norms must consequently favour children who have been taught through a phonic approach.

Some examiners may deem it advisable to test spelling and arithmetic attainments. With certain children this is desirable; for example, children who are failing in reading often have average or above-average attainments in arithmetic. This is useful diagnostic information because it may suggest that the child's difficulties in reading are related to specific disabilities in one or more reading skills or that the principal problem in reading is one of poor motivation due to environmental factors such as language deprivation or the use of inappropriate teaching methods.

Personality; case history and background information; organization of diagnostic examination

1 *Tests of personality*

Some examiners, particularly those working in a clinical rather than school setting, may wish to include tests of personality in the diagnostic programme. We do not feel that they are an essential part of the programme. An assessment of the child's personality and emotional development are very important, but an examiner should be able to arrive at a reliable picture of these through his contact with the child during the psychological testing already described, and from information supplied at the time of referral. From testing and background

[1] J. C. Daniels and H. Diack, *The Standard Reading Tests* (Chatto and Windus: London 1960).

evidence information should accrue about the child's emotional development, his relationships with adults and other children, his reactions to failure, his frustration tolerance, his work habits and degree of persistence and determination, any neurotic or psychotic manifestations, and the level of social competence.

2 *Case history and background information*[1]

At some stage in the diagnosis a comprehensive history of the child should be compiled. This should include the following:

1 Any evidence about pre-natal, peri-natal and post-natal difficulties. The following appear to be significant:

- *a* Mother had poor health during pregnancy.
- *b* Blood incompatibility and Rh factor.
- *c* Mother had severe emotional difficulty during pregnancy.
- *d* Mother had serious fall during pregnancy.
- *e* Mother had difficulties in pregnancies, e.g. miscarriages, bleeding, premature births, or high blood pressure.
- *f* Toxaemia of pregnancy.
- *g* Long labour—over 36 hours.
- *h* Premature birth—less than 7 months' gestation or birth weight under 5 lb.
- *i* Precipitate birth; dry birth.
- Large baby—over 10 lb.
- *k* Breech or Caesarean delivery.
- *l* Anoxia reported.
- *m* Baby transfused or jaundiced.
- *n* Feeding difficulties—baby did not suck well and was 'lazy' and inactive.
- *o* Baby exceptionally good—'We did not know we had him; he was such a good baby.'
- *p* Baby not wanted—attempted abortion.

[1] A. E. Tansley, 'Studying Children "At Risk"', *Special Education*, vol. LV, no. 1, 1966.

q Mother over 40 years old when baby born and long gap since previous pregnancy.
r Baby had many illnesses in first three years; recurrent bronchitis, measles with high temperature (105°+), meningitis, encephalitis.
s Brain injury due to falls resulting in unconsciousness.
t Disturbed sleep rhythms in early infancy.
u History of severe convulsions or 'fits'.
v Early separation of mother and baby.

2 Evidence of subnormality, mental illness, or reading disability in the family history.

3 Other factors in the family, e.g. parental disharmony, sibling rivalry, child is 'odd man' in an otherwise normal family; family broken.

4 The child's reactions to school as indicated by parents and school reports. Of particular importance is a report about the child's response to any remedial education which may have been tried.

5 Any evidence of behaviour difficulties at home and in school; truancy, social difficulties, delinquent tendencies.

3 The organization of the diagnostic examination

A comprehensive diagnosis is dependent upon inter-disciplinary co-operation since doctors, psychologists, teachers and social workers may be involved. It is a 'team' effort, but one member of the team should act as co-ordinator. If the diagnosis is made in a school setting, it is preferable that the head teacher should undertake this function. He should also act as convener for arranging Case Conferences.

One of the greatest difficulties in arranging a diagnostic programme is to know where to begin, and what investigations are necessary before treatment should start. There can, of course, be no rigid programme; each child should be considered individually. In very few instances will it be necessary to use all the examinations and tests we have described and suggested. There are always the dangers that far too much time may be wasted on trying to disclose the aetiological factors and that tests may be used simply to complete a diagnostic schedule in a systematic way. The sooner treatment begins the better for all concerned; indeed, the child's lack of response to systematic treatment is often the best guide to the diagnostic information which should be sought. In practice, this means that the remedial teacher (or educational psychologist) should be the key figure in the early stages; he should be sufficiently well trained to be able to suggest which items in the full diagnostic programme should be used initially.

The priority given to the various tests and examinations, and the order of presentation will vary according to the circumstances. They will depend upon the age of the child, the intensity and character of presenting symptoms, the time available, information received from other sources, and the examiner's experience. The following order is given only as a guide and is based on our experience of older (9+ years) cases of acute reading disability. From the order, it will be noted that we are influenced by our conclusion that, in many cases, acute failure in reading is indicative of neurological abnormality or immaturity, perceptual-motor difficulty and language retardation or anomaly, and combinations of these.

1 General appraisal of the child's language development, motor efficiency and constructive and imaginative play during the establishing of rapport.

2 Test of ability to draw the Standard Figures and a man.

3 Tests of lateral dominance.

4 If 2 and 3 indicate visuo-motor and visuo-spatial difficulties, then apply all the perceptual-motor tests mentioned earlier.

5 Test of auditory rhythm and sequencing.

6 If the above indicate neurological disorganization, then request a neurological examination and, if possible, an electroencephalogram (E.E.G. examination).

7 Tests of language development, e.g. English Picture Vocabulary Test (E.P.V.T.).

8 If 7 suggests language/speech problems, then give the I.T.P.A. Test and, if necessary, tests of aphasia.

9 If the child can read at all, give the Neale Analysis of Reading Ability battery of tests, or the Diack and Daniels tests.

10 Assess level of intelligence using W.I.S.C. or Raven Matrices/Vocabulary Tests.

11 Explore the case history with particular reference to the factors mentioned earlier as being of significance.

12 Medical examination with particular emphasis on eyes and ears. It is usually advisable for all children to have an audiometric examination.

13 If thought necessary, tests of personality and psychiatric examination.

Some examiners may feel that the greatest priority should be given to assessing the child's intellectual level by using the W.I.S.C. However, they should bear in mind what was said about this test on p. 120. The child's responses should be examined closely to see how far they indicate other lines of investigation, e.g. into perceptual and language development, and the type of remediation required.

Systematic recording of diagnostic information is, of course, essential and a suggested Diagnostic Assessment Record Sheet as used in St. Francis Residential School is given in Appendix 1 on p. 157. It will be observed that no space is given for the results of medical and psychiatric examinations. This is because the school keeps separate records for these, and they are readily available to those concerned in diagnosis and education; outstanding features are noted in the Case History section. It will be appreciated that the Record Sheet is used primarily to provide a quick and easily assessed diagnostic record; fuller information is available in the completed individual test schedules and reports.

11 Remedial treatment of acute reading disability

Introduction

The use of the term *remedial* is often questioned by teachers involved in helping failing children. Some authorities have suggested the use of the word *re-education* since talk of remediation suggests medical or even pathological associations. However, we use the term remedial because the treatment given (educational, psychological, medical and social) is directly related to a scientific diagnosis of reading disability. To use the term re-education would seem appropriate only when the cause of failure is confined to remedying the adverse effects of faulty methods, techniques and approaches. This type of failure is normally cured by the use of good, normal teaching for the individual child because it is not due to any psychological or physical abnormality and hardly deserves the description of acute disability. Thus many children we have treated have responded quickly to the use of the method described earlier in this book; their reading failure has been due to inefficient teaching. Our remedial cases are children who have failed to respond to our reading programme and adaptations and modification of it to suit individual needs. The methods to be described in Chapter 12 will, of course, be applicable to and useful in helping some of these children over particular difficulties; for instance, when emotional problems or neurotic manifestations inhibit the child from responding successfully to parts of the programme unless new materials or an intensification of approach and extended practice are used; or again, when sufficient attention has not been given to developmental readiness and the psycholinguistic and other processes involved in reading have become temporarily disturbed or disorganized.

It may be thought that all reading failure is due to bad, untimely teaching. However, this is obviously a dangerous line to take and experience quickly demonstrates how fallacious it is. It is dangerous because teachers who believe it are usually too involved and if they fail they rationalize by calling the child lazy or too lacking in intelligence; it is fallacious because we now know that, for a variety of reasons, some children do not develop normally and are thus atypical. It is for these children that remedial education based on thorough diagnosis is essential; they are unable to respond to good teaching, coaching or re-education in reading and need expert help.

A theoretical basis for remedial treatment

To have any real chance of resulting in success, remedial treatment must have direction and purpose, and must be undertaken by specially trained people. Throughout this book we have stressed the neurophysiological and psychoneurological processes involved in learning to read. Some knowledge of these seems to be essential. In this connection we have been guided by the work of Hebb[1] and Lise Gellner.[2] Hebb's theory of learning, based on a neuropsychological approach, has greatly influenced the work in the author's school in general, and its remedial department in particular. This is not the place to embark on a lengthy description and discussion of Hebb's theory. Briefly, he conceived of learning as being very much dependent upon a healthy central nervous system which is able

[1] D. O. Hebb, *The Organization of Behaviour* (John Wiley: New York 1949).
[2] Op. cit.

to accept, analyse, integrate, structure and give meaning to information received by sensory receptors. He is concerned with neurological and perceptual function; the transmission of energy along neural pathways; the processes involved in this transmission (for instance, cell-firing and changes in synaptic structure and function); cell assemblies, as he calls them, and combinations of these as the basic mechanism in sensory and perceptual-motor activity; excitation and inhibition of cells and cell assemblies; causes of failure in the central nervous system. It is, of course, impossible to verify his theory directly, but is in accord with current knowledge of brain physiology; it appears to give reasonable answers to many of the problems which other theories of learning leave unsolved. It certainly appears to have exciting implications for educational theory and practice. For our present purposes, it indicates that remedial treatment in reading should be organized around the following tentative suggestions.

1 Initially, methods should involve as much of the cortex as possible to assist the firing of cell assemblies over a wide area.

2 From 1 it follows that early training should be based on objects rather than symbols and that a multi-sensory approach should be used.

3 Attention should be given to the type, form and intensity of stimuli used. With young children large, well-designed, distinct, visual stimuli and clear, well-articulated sounds are necessary. Much experiment and research are still needed in this connection.

4 In order to establish interfacilitation between cell assemblies, systematic practice and drill are essential.

5 Developmental readiness is vital. Thus simpler cell structures must be built before more complex ones can arise.

6 Language will be important in exciting and inhibiting cell activity in the absence of direct receptor stimulation.

7 Programming of learning situations will be essential.

Learning must be guided, controlled and made explicit in the early stages. This implies that training may be needed to clarify sensory experiences.

8 Neural pathways which are more easily established should be used to develop those which are difficult. Thus, remedial methods should make use of strong neural links to improve weak ones, and eventually result in compensation through new linkages in intact cells.

9 Movement, which involves the motor areas of the cortex, plays an important part in cell-assembly connections. Thus, in some instances, children may learn quicker by using stimuli which move, or appear to move, rather than static ones.

Lise Gellner stresses the importance of subcortical damage in causing disturbances in integrative processes. She states that cortical damage is probably not a cause of learning difficulty but is due to lack of receptor stimulation which results in a lack of cortical development. Thus, she cites how blind and deaf people of normal intelligence have visual and auditory areas of the cortex undeveloped. She is primarily concerned with visual and auditory disturbances and postulates four types of learning difficulty:

1 Visuo-somatic or *movement blindness*—children with this difficulty cannot imitate movement, match forms, copy visual patterns, and 'use the hands under control of the eyes'.

2 Visuo-autonomic or *meaning blindness*, but not movement blindness. The clinical picture of this type includes reduced visual impulse, difficulty in looking at stationary forms, rapid variations in responses to visual stimuli, great desire to explore with touch, distractibility and overactivity.

3 Auditory-somatic or *sound deafness* although hearing is intact. Here, children cannot give a movement response

to sound stimulation, e.g. they have difficulty in reproducing sounds, and in miming.

4 Auditory-autonomic or *word-meaning deafness*. This disability does not affect speech development and memory for sounds is usually very good. However, it results in an inability to answer questions, which can result in lack of communication, mutism, pseudo-intellectual subnormality and grave emotional problems.

Much more research and experiment are required to substantiate Gellner's theory. However, together with Hebb's theory, it does underline what has been said earlier, viz., reading is a psychoneurological process and any structural or mechanical damage to or disturbance in the neural pathways which are involved will lead to specific symptoms and necessitate special types of remediation. It stresses the importance of viewing neurological abnormality and sensory and perceptual disturbance as being of much greater importance than low I.Q. in both diagnosis and treatment. Reading disability should therefore be viewed as a symptom not a clinical entity.

Other considerations in treatment

Many of the principles already given as being of importance will, of course, be important in remedial education. If some of them are repeated here it is simply to stress their importance in helping to cure reading disability and to eradicate or ameliorate the distress which it causes.

1 *A good relationship between teacher and child is essential*: education should be based on empathy and take place in an atmosphere of hope, calm, pleasant co-operation, and consistency.

2 *Treatment should begin as early as possible*. This is important because:

a difficulties in perception occur more frequently in young children and if they are not put right may persist and eventually lead to an incurable disability, say, at the secondary stage of education;

b it is likely that neural pathways can be more easily facilitated in young children when the central nervous system is in a more flexible, malleable state. Even with children who show a developmental lag, treatment should not be too long delayed if compensations are to occur;

c faulty habits and attitudes may be avoided;

d language, intellectual, and emotional development may not be so adversely affected.

3 Younger reading failures will need an abundance of sensori-motor and language experience.

4 A comprehensive approach is necessary; rarely will success be achieved by using one method or technique. Often the attack will have to be based on a multi-discipline approach.

5 Developing readiness must be viewed as a necessary function of remedial work. The order and different rates at which processes and abilities develop must be appreciated.

6 It may be necessary to eradicate previous faulty learning by a process of re-education.

7 Education should take place through intact neural links and abilities and lead to compensations for or improvements in those which are weak.

8 A naïve symptomatic approach is often doomed to failure. This follows from 7 above, e.g. if the symptomatology indicates poor visual discrimination, to train or give practice in this alone is usually inadequate.

9 Routines must be simple and well-structured.

10 Treatment must be consistent and regular.

11 When in doubt about which method to use, make a

multi-sensory attack using visual, auditory, tactile and kinaesthetic links supported by spoken language.

12 A remedial programme should be devised for each child but, where possible, group teaching should be used and children should be encouraged to help one another.

12 Remedial techniques and methods

An attempt will now be made to make suggestions about specific approaches, methods and techniques to be used in relation to diagnostic information:

Programme of activities when diagnostic assessment reveals neurological abnormality and acute perceptual-motor disturbance

Exercises to hasten neurological organization

These may include the following, many of which are based on the suggestions made by Kephart:[1]

1 *A variety of balancing and postural activities*

a Walking along a line painted on the floor.
b Walking along a piece of wood about 1 in. thick, 2 to 3 in. wide and 10 ft. long.
c Walking along a balance bench or beam at varying heights.

The walking should include forward, backward, turning and

[1] N. C. Kephart, *The Slow Learner in the Classroom* (Charles E. Merril Books: Columbus, Ohio 1960).

sideways movements. To assist balance, the child should be encouraged to talk to himself, e.g. 'forward, forward', 'backward, backward', 'right, right', 'left, left', and to move slowly, smoothly, and with good posture.

Balancing on a balance board (2 ft. × 2 ft. and raised by central blocks of varying heights); while balancing on the board, catching a ball thrown to the child from varying angles and distances, or bouncing and catching a ball himself. While balancing on this board, the child may also have ocular pursuit training, i.e. watching a target moving in a variety of directions or trying to hit or touch a moving target.

2 *Duplicating demonstrated body positions and movements* when demonstrator is first turned away from and later facing the child. *In cases of difficulty*, the child should be encouraged to talk about what is happening, e.g. 'right arm out, now down to my side', etc. However, this should be dispensed with as soon as possible.

3 *Responding to spoken directions* in relation to body movement (the aim here is to develop improved ideas of body image and structure, directional orientation, posture, controlled movement and cerebral dominance), e.g. raise your right arm, touch your right ear with your right hand, touch your left knee with your right foot, etc. Have the child lie down on the floor and ask him to perform various combinations of movements. With young children bilateral movements should be practised but when right or left dominance is being established emphasis should be given to strengthening the preferred side.

4 *Moving the body through a variety of obstacles*; crawling under, stepping over, passing between, passing through obstacles with increasing difficulty in the form of obstruction. The following examples will illustrate the types of activity involved:

a Walking between two jumping stands, eventually leaving only sufficient space for the child to pass between with sideways movements; the child is asked to estimate the space through which he can move.

b Crawling under a horizontal bar which is progressively lowered to increase the difficulty.

c Crawling through hoops or tyres of varying diameter.

For all these exercises which are designed to improve body image and the exploration of extra-body space, the child should wear a minimum of clothing so that if he touches an obstacle he can feel, and name, the part of the body which touched the obstacle.

5 *Visuo-motor integration exercises* similar to those described in Chapter 10, p. 94.

6 *Training in memorizing and performing a sequence of movements* either demonstrated or given verbally. Children who find this difficult will probably have to be blindfolded and the teacher will have to move the child's limbs and then ask the child to repeat the movements.

7 *Stepping on stepping-stones* (or foot marks painted on the floor) which are marked to indicate which foot has to be placed on which stone, e.g. stones painted red for the right foot and blue for the left foot. The stones are placed in positions such that the size of step varies and the child has to move through angles and, in some cases, cross one leg over the other.

8 *Training in rhythmic movement and memorizing rhythms* tapped, sung or played on a percussion instrument (see Chapter 3).

9 *Musical, singing or other games* which involve the appreciation of body parts and the use of rhythmic movements.

10 *Dramatic activities* with particular emphasis on miming sensations, feelings, common experiences, and imaginary situations; for instance, miming fear, anger, pleasure, sorrow, surprise; miming having a bath, eating hot food or cold ice cream; miming a visit to the circus, North Pole, African jungle, etc.

The creative teacher, who appreciates the important part

which movement plays in perceptual and conceptual development and learning generally, will be able to amplify and improve upon the above suggestions.

It may be appropriate here to describe briefly the theory put forward by Delacato[1] and his associates. His theory is not yet generally accepted and much more experimental work and evidence are needed. However, our limited experience in applying his ideas to the treatment of acute reading disability and brain damage leads to the conclusion that the theory must not be dismissed lightly. The theory is based on the following ideas and observations:

1 Man differs from all other beings in cellular organization and cellular function.

2 Man should be unilateral, i.e. one brain hemisphere should be definitely dominant. This dominant hemisphere usually controls language skills.

3 Remedial reading should not begin until central neurological organization has been thoroughly achieved and cerebral hemisphere dominance has been established.

4 For children who have not reached the unilaterality stage, a programme of neurological re-education should be undertaken. This should begin at the developmental level at which the child is able to function normally and lead to firmly established cerebral dominance and unilaterality in handedness, footedness and eyedness.

The progression in neurological re-education follows the ontogenetic developmental stages in normal neurological growth. Thus in developing mobility at the cerebral dominance level the child progresses from random movements of arms and legs to crawling homolaterally (ipsilateral movement of arm and leg), cross-pattern crawling (contralateral movement of arm and leg), homolateral creeping, cross-pattern creeping, cross-pattern walking, running, and use of dominant leg in kicking and balancing.

[1] C. H. Delacato, *The Diagnosis and Treatment of Speech and Reading Problems* (Charles C. Thomas: Springfield, Ill. 1963).

In treatment, the child's level of mobility is determined and training is then given to hasten development through the remaining stages. These stages in mobility are related to the growth of the central nervous system from the spinal cord, to the medulla, pons, mid-brain and cortical levels. They are paralleled by developments in language, manual dexterity and visual, auditory and tactile competence. In the majority of children the growth process, culminating in lateral dominance, language and conceptual competence, reading, complete speech skills and tactile efficiency, is reached at between 7 and 8 years of age.

Pre-reading programmes must therefore include exercises designed to encourage neurological organization and function. These exercises should be related to the child's level of neurological development as revealed in diagnosis. To assist in achieving this relationship, Delacato and his associates provide a Developmental Profile and give detailed instructions of how treatment should be carried out.

Teachers wishing to attempt using this method should bear in mind the following considerations.

1 It is still perhaps too early to accept the hypothesis that complete cerebral dominance is of such fundamental importance in relation to the beginnings of teaching reading skills.

2 When laterality is being trained, particularly in developing a dominant eye, co-operation with doctors is required. For example, Delacato suggests that the sub-dominant eye should be occluded until the dominant eye has been trained. This has obvious inherent dangers in relation to visual acuity, depth perception (stereopsis) and binocular vision. Again, since tonality and musical skills appear to be centred in the subdominant hemisphere, all music has to be cut out in order to make the subdominant hemisphere as quiescent as possible; this can be a serious decision to make.

3 In many children it is not always possible to make an unequivocal decision about which hemisphere should be

trained to assume the dominant role. As stated earlier, we use the Harris Tests of Lateral Dominance; the results are often so confusing that a diagnosis of lateral dominance is difficult. This is particularly so with regard to eyedness which is so very often the odd-man-out, i.e. children's eyedness is often opposed to handedness and footedness. Furthermore, many of these mixed-dominance children are good readers, or if they are bad readers, respond satisfactorily to reading coaching and remediation. Delacato emphasizes, however, that for older children whose laterality is confused treatment should begin at the mid-brain level (e.g. training in crawling, development of good tactile sensation, language usage). How far this is desirable or necessary is open to doubt.

4 Speech defects are claimed to be related to confused laterality. It is suggested that while neurological training is taking place, speech training should be stopped. Stutterers should have bilateral function reinforced first and then move to unilateral training. These suggestions, though perhaps theoretically sound in that they attempt to deal with central causes before peripheral treatment begins, must obviously be applied cautiously—there is a danger of increasing emotional tension and no sure guarantee that improvements will necessarily result.

5 Doman,[1] one of Delacato's collaborators, is now claiming to be able to teach babies *to read*. This does not square with the psychoneurological hypothesis unless he can produce irrefutable evidence that training has so hastened neurological development that lateral dominance can be achieved very much earlier.

We are not yet in a position to evaluate reliably the results of the work described above. There are grounds, however, for cautious optimism because some children are now already responding more successfully to our remedial or

[1] G. Doman, *How to Teach Your Baby to Read* (Random House: New York 1965).

normal reading programme than previously. We cannot say, however, that this is solely due to the effect of the exercises (including Delacato exercises) being used. We are, however, certain that a remedial reading programme must include appropriate physical exercises as an integral part.

Exercises to hasten sensory channel integration and perceptual-motor development

If the diagnosis reveals that the child has difficulty in integrating sensory stimuli through visual, auditory, tactile or kinaesthetic channels, then appropriate training is necessary. It is extremely rare to find a child in whom all channels are defective; our experience is quite wide but we have not come across such a child. Training should therefore begin by using those channels which are intact. One example will serve to illustrate the form which training may take.

A child of 9 years of age is completely illiterate. Tests reveal that he has a significant verbal bias on the W.I.S.C. despite a slight speech defect, good auditory abilities on the I.T.P.A., and he can identify objects haptically; he is unable to draw the eight standard figures beyond, say, a circle; all visual scores on the I.T.P.A. are low; kinaesthetic-haptic and kinaesthetic-visual channel integration are deficient; his drawing of a man reveals poor motor ability and immature ideas of his body image and schema; his laterality has not been established; motor encoding is low on I.T.P.A. This information therefore suggests that:

1 His strong neural links are auditory and tactile.

2 His language development is reasonably good and should be used in facilitating new links.

3 His weak neural links are visual and motor.

Success in reading will be impossible until he can overcome or compensate for his visual difficulties. Strong auditory perception will not lead to success until he can relate auditory to visual symbols. His individual remedial programme will therefore have to be organized on the following lines:

1 He should have ample opportunity in play for sensori-motor experiences.

2 Training should be given in neurological organization on the lines already indicated, with particular emphasis on visuo-motor activities.

3 He should receive specific training in haptic-visual integration, making use of language to help the transfer of haptic information to develop visual perception. This training may have to be very explicit. For example, whilst exploring a triangle haptically his fingers will have to be guided, and language used to heighten haptic appreciation: he will feel the three straight sides, the three sharp corners, long and short sides, and talk about these as he explores the triangle fully. He will then be asked to try to identify the triangle visually by choosing from three drawn figures which, at first, include two markedly different from the triangle to be identified. If he still cannot find the triangle his tactile ability, plus language, will be used to explore the drawing of the triangle. Patient training on these lines will lead to improvements in haptic-visual integration particularly if his training is well-programmed.

4 He should receive specific training in haptic-kinaesthetic and kinaesthetic-visual integration on similar lines to the above.

5 He should receive perceptual training on those exercises in the perceptual training programme which are designed to improve perceptual-motor ability, e.g. hand–eye co-ordination, visual copying, visual discrimination and visual sequencing.

6 His auditory memory should be used to improve visual memory and visual sequencing. For example, using a selection of pictures, the teacher names some of them and the child places them in the order named.

7 He should have ample opportunities to mime.

8 He should trace words in sand saying the whole word as he traces.

9 With improvements in visual-motor perception he should begin to classify and match objects and shapes; match word to word, word to object and picture.

If his disabilities are severe, all this training will extend over a long period (in some of our cases, two years). It is rare that progress is not eventually made. Indeed, when compensatory links begin to work, surprising progress often occurs. It is as though 'the penny drops' by magic.

Individual remedial programmes such as this are necessary for every child, dependent upon his strengths and weaknesses in those processes involved in perceptual-motor development. The remaining part of the chapter will describe some such programmes to overcome other types of disability.

Programme of activities when the diagnostic assessment reveals visual perception difficulties

These difficulties will have revealed themselves in many ways which will include poor form perception and visual copying, right-left confusion, high error and distortion scores on the Benton Visual Retention Test, immature Bender Gestalt drawings, low I.T.P.A. scores in visual decoding, visual-motor association and visual-motor sequencing, and a Raven Progressive Matrices percentile ranking which is highly discrepant with verbal test results.

Specific educational treatment may have to be delayed until a full visual acuity and, if necessary, ophthalmological examination has been carried out and corrective measures taken. If visual difficulties are also accompanied by poor motor ability the likelihood of brain injury must be considered.

The form of remedial treatment will again depend upon which neural links, or sense modalities, are strong. It will be through using these that compensation for or correction of visual weaknesses will be achieved. Certainly, substantial reading progress is impossible until the visual problems have been resolved or ameliorated. The use of an auditory-kinaesthetic-tactile method will reveal which of these three sensory modalities are functioning more or less normally. These normal channels, mediated by the use of spoken language, should be used to draw attention to and assist in the analysis and synthesis of visual stimuli.

The following exercises and activities, or appropriate selections from them, have proved useful:

1. Training in visual copying, visual discrimination, visual sequencing, visual rhythms, and temporal sequencing such as that described in Chapter 3.
2. Training in form perception, visuo-motor and visuo-haptic integration.
3. Making use of a programmed series of jigsaws and picture-matching exercises using language to heighten appreciation of form.
4. Recognizing objects or pictures presented visually, varying from simple naming to describing actions or scenes, detecting mutilations (e.g. what is missing?) and absurdities (why is this picture wrong or silly?).
5. Finding objects or pictures when given a name or verbal description.
6. Classifying objects when given the initial sound they begin with.
7. Putting objects or pictures in a given order which has previously been given orally.
8. Training in visual analysis and synthesis. For example:

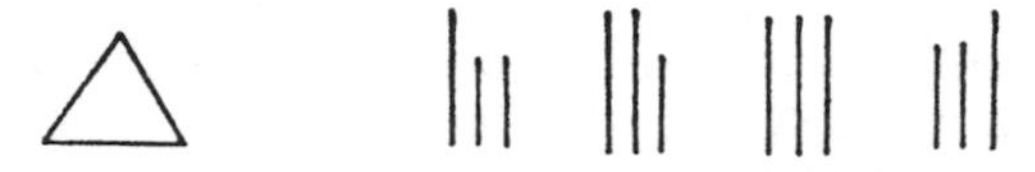

Which of these groups of lines (or sticks) will make the figure?

Which of these will finish the circle? etc., etc.

Make a piece of card with a slit in it and slide the card at varying speeds over a picture or figure. Ask the child to identify the picture or figure either when the whole or part of the figure has been passed over.

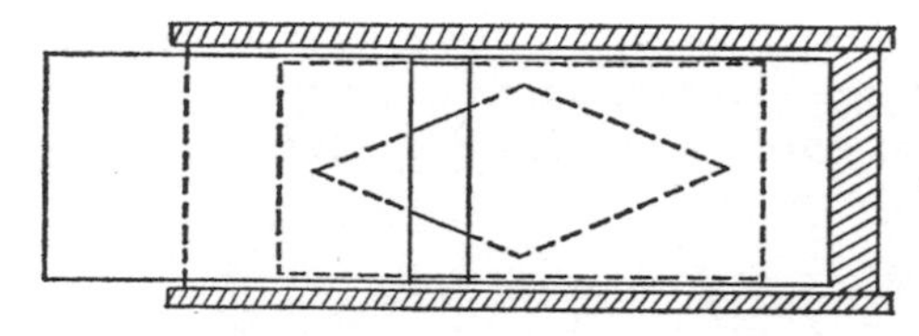

Slot moves over the figure always in a left–right direction.

9 If auditory perception and motor rhythmic abilities are good, begin to teach reading by a sound-writing approach. Begin by teaching the most frequent consonants and vowels first. As the child writes or traces the letter he should say the letter, completing the sound as he completes the first movement in writing. Proceed to two-letter blending running the sounds together so that the blend is completed by the end of the first movement in the second letter. Follow this with three-letter blends. During this training encourage the child to find what he has written from a visual selection of letters, blends or words.

10 When the child has progressed to writing simple nouns, verbs, adjectives and prepositions, encourage him to do word-picture and word-word matching exercises.

11 Use the apparatus described in 8 to encourage the left-right visual scanning and blending of words.

12 When the child can read a few words, write these on individual cards, say a short sentence to him, and ask him

to find the right cards and place them in order to make the sentence, e.g.

my	*house*	*is*	*big*

13 The method used by Grace Fernald[1] may be used as a later development of the above exercises. This is described in full in her book but the following brief description will illustrate how the method relates to the suggestions given above.

The child tells the teacher what he would like to read about and the topic is discussed. The teacher may suggest the first sentence and the child tries to write it. Any word the child cannot write or read is studied in the following way:

a The word is written in large script by the teacher either on a card or in a large alphabet-indexed book. The card or book must be placed some distance from the child's own teaching space.

b Away from his teaching space, the child traces the word *with finger contact*, saying the word aloud or to himself as he tries to establish the connection between sound and form. *The vocalization of the word should be natural and smooth*, and not over-emphasize individual letter-sounds or syllables. In longer words, syllables should be vocalized as they are traced. For example, Fernald gives the example of the word *important*. The child should say *im* as he writes the first syllable, *por* as he writes the second syllable, and *tant* for the third syllable. Finger contact should be maintained until the whole word has been traced and the three syllables should be blended to keep the sound pattern of the whole word intact.

c Tracing should continue until the child feels he can move to his desk and write the word on a piece of

[1] G. Fernald, *Remedial Techniques in Basic Subjects* (McGraw-Hill: New York 1943).

paper. He writes the word and then takes his copy to compare it with the one he has traced. If his copy is correct he writes it in his book (as part of his own written story) without reference to his copy. If his copy is incorrect the tracing operation is repeated until accuracy is established.

d Every word the child is unable to write or read is learned by the above method. The movement from the tracing book to the child's desk is very important.

e Tracing with finger contact is abandoned as soon as the child is capable of managing without it. For instance, he may practise writing the word from the example and then see if he can write it independently. The writing must still be accompanied by normal vocalization of the word.

f The child's auditory abilities should be used to help him to appreciate the visual similarities between words which have similar sound patterns, e.g. words which begin or end with the same sound and symbol.

g At the end of each lesson what the child has written should be typed so that he reads his story in typescript as well as in his own handwriting.

The Fernald method is often useful with older non-readers whose motor development is such that they can write easily. It is, however, less appropriate for younger children with immature or poor hand–eye co-ordination. However, for them the method may be adapted to omit writing and to place more emphasis on kinaesthetic-tactile senses. Thus, a word which the child cannot read may be traced with finger contact (either on paper or in sand) to help him to memorize it on visual presentation. It should be remembered that some children may never learn to write legibly and for them a typewriter should be used as a substitute for their handwriting. In using this remedial method, care should be taken to ensure:

a that vocalization of words being traced and written should not become unnatural lest the child's reading should become too phonic or almost alphabetic. When the method was first used in the author's school insufficient care was taken over this aspect and although progress was made initially it was not maintained because of too great an insistence on the part of the child to read alphabetically or phonically;

b that the child, in selecting the vocabulary for his story, should not introduce too many difficult words too quickly. The teacher should encourage the child to match his aspirations to his abilities. Indeed, it may be advisable for the teacher to programme the child's reading to ensure good grading, adequate repetition and a satisfactory balance between phonically regular and irregular words.

For children with visual difficulties it would seem obvious that a reading scheme with a phonic bias should be used. The Initial Teaching Alphabet system may be useful because it is phonically more regular than traditional orthography and there might be less confusion in relating sound to visual patterns. However, because of visual difficulties the transfer from I.T.A. to traditional symbols may be more difficult. The Diack and Daniels Royal Road Readers[1] may also be appropriate for this type of child. However, a phonic scheme used in isolation without remedial work to overcome visual problems is not likely to succeed with children who have acute visual perception disabilities, because reading is primarily a visual process.

In devising methods to overcome visual difficulties the two types of visual disturbance described by Gellner should be borne in mind. The *visual-somatic group* can learn to read without much difficulty provided they are allowed to hold the book and move it as they wish. Their peripheral vision is usually affected, as seen in their staring gaze, and visual stimuli have to be manœuvred to bring them to central-vision positions. They have difficulty in moving and adjusting their eyes to scan visual stimuli and compensate by moving the source

[1] J. C. Daniels and H. Diack, *The Royal Road Readers* (Chatto and Windus: London 1957).

of stimulation itself. They should not therefore be presented with long lines of print because they will have difficulty in attention and concentration if they have too great a preoccupation with adjusting their angles of vision either by head movements or moving the book to bring words into the central-vision area of the retina. The slotted–card device may be useful in teaching them; however, *the slot should be kept stationary* in front of their eyes and the words should be moved into the aperture. One further observation is worthy of mention—these children like colour, and if visual memory is weak colour cues may be helpful.

The visual-autonomic group are quite different. They are interested in movement and have difficulty in dealing with static visual stimuli; they have poor visual memories and great difficulty in attention. They are hyperactive and distractible; colour disturbs them. The children in this group need a predominantly phonic approach similar to that already described in this chapter.

Programme of activities when the diagnostic assessment reveals auditory perception difficulties

In the case of children with auditory difficulties the initial diagnostic assessment may reveal some or all of the following: poor automatic language levels; performance bias on the W.I.S.C.; speech defects which reveal inability to distinguish between certain consonantal sounds; low scores on auditory sub-tests of the I.T.P.A.; symptoms of receptive and/or expressive aphasia; poor auditory rhythm, memory and sequencing; unilateral or bilateral hearing loss on audiometer test; evidence of recurrent catarrh or upper-respiratory infections.

Treatment for these children may have to be delayed until a full audiological examination has been carried out and corrective measures taken; the removal of tonsils and adenoids may also be necessary. Remedial teaching in reading may have to be accompanied by speech therapy and an intensive language programme to improve automatic language facility and auditory discrimination. The remedial reading programme should be based on the following suggestions:

1 If the visual, kinaesthetic and tactile pathways are intact, these children should be able to learn by a sight approach when these pathways are sufficiently developed for reading readiness. Much use should be made of writing and/or tracing. In the early stages teaching should be based on a silent reading approach, particularly if there is a severe speech defect. To ensure that reading for meaning is taking place, written comprehension exercises should be given if the child can write without too much difficulty. Our experience of children with auditory difficulties indicates that many of them have good motor abilities and writing should therefore be encouraged and used. If writing is difficult, however, comprehension may be tested by asking the child to draw, make or mime what he has read. If the speech defect is not too severe, the child can talk about the content of his reading.

2 Since the child finds the acquisition of a sight vocabulary fairly easy, good motivation is present initially and helps the child to tackle auditory problems later. However, when auditory disabilities are acute the early enthusiasm can later give way to frustration, non-co-operation, restlessness and severe behaviour problems. It is essential, therefore, that during the time the sight vocabulary is developing the teacher should use a systematic programme of preparation for the time when continuing reading progress is dependent upon the use of auditory discrimination and perception. The observant teacher will have noticed during the early, successful stage that the child has auditory difficulties (even if partial deafness is not diagnosed). The child will mispronounce certain consonants, be unable to remember what has been read visually, misunderstand instructions and directions, give inappropriate answers to questions, show little awareness of the association of visual symbol and sound, and confuse letters and words which sound nearly alike. He may omit suffixes or

final letters and his spoken language may be ungrammatical.

3 The programme designed for hastening auditory and language readiness (see Chapter 3, section 10, Chapter 5 and Chapter 6) should include the following activities and exercises.

a Listening to recordings (on a tape recorder) of familiar sounds (running water, sawing, telephone bell, clock chime, clock ticking, different voices, animal noises, etc.) and either matching sounds to pictures or saying what they are.
b Naming objects or pictures of objects, leading to describing a picture in full.
c Repeating sentences accurately, gradually increasing the length of sentence to be repeated; learning nursery rhymes and jingles.
d Showing a series of pictures to the child then removing them and asking him to name them in order.
e Carrying out instructions and directions.
f Practising telephone conversations and dialling numbers given verbally.
g Practice in giving appropriate answers to questions.
h Miming actions described verbally.
i Giving opposites, e.g. what is the opposite of *hot*?
j Giving practice in pronouncing words and listening to sounds in speech.
k Recognizing objects or actions described orally.
l Classification exercises; classifying things according to colour, texture, size, use and shape; classifying objects, pictures and words according to their initial, ending, or middle sounds.
m Discrimination exercises in which the child is asked to choose the appropriate word from a selection of words which are similar in sound or form, e.g.

The light was bright/bite
Thing/thin/think before you act.

Many of the exercises used in the 'Sound Sense' books[1] are useful in this context, if given orally.

n Making sentences out of jumbled, individual words presented on cards or given orally.

o Putting in missing words.

p Changing the tense of a sentence to improve the use of present and past participles.

q Changing words or sentences from singular to plural and vice versa.

4 Children with auditory difficulties and speech defects often require exercises to improve balance and posture, establish cerebral dominance, and develop auditory rhythm. They are often deficient in balance and/or rhythmic ability and require training in these. Some are extremely good in balance and can be quite graceful in movement; however, they cannot move rhythmically to a given rhythm or to music. The integration of auditory and kinaesthetic inputs is disturbed. Improvements can be affected by tapping the rhythm on the child's body as he moves or by assisted movement of limbs in time with rhythm. The strength of the tapping or the degree of assistance in movement should be gradually reduced until finally the child moves more rhythmically without help.

5 A programme of exercises is generally needed to improve auditory memory. Many of the exercises in 3 will be of help in this. If visual and tactile memories are good they should be used in an attempt to improve memory for sound sequences. For example, show the child a series of pictures and then ask him to give the sequence from memory verbally; let him feel (while blindfolded) a series of objects and when he has felt them all name them in order.

6 Give specific training in blending sounds orally and then with visual presentation. Many children with auditory impairments have difficulty in blending from left to right

[1] Op. cit.

even when the individual sounds are known. The greater the effort they make the more rigid they become and they appear completely unable to remember the individual sounds in sequence. They are unable to give the first or last sounds in, say, a three-letter word. We have found that in addition to the techniques suggested for phonic instruction, the following devices are useful:

a Give the child a short sentence orally and ask him to 'write' it using flashcards. Discuss which word is first, last or in the middle.

b Use the slotted card to scan words while blending is being taught. The slot should be only wide enough to reveal one letter at a time; as the slot moves from one letter to the next the child should be helped to blend. The movement of the slot should gradually be speeded up so that blending quickens and rigidity is reduced.

Card slides over word in this direction.

This device may also be used to encourage phrase reading and memory for phrases. It is also a great help in improving attention and concentration.

7 The use of a sound-tracing method may be helpful when auditory analysis becomes necessary. Marion Monroe[1] describes this method in detail and gives a programme of exercises designed to increase the association between visual symbol and sound and to improve the differentiation of sounds.

As mentioned earlier, Lise Gellner differentiates two groups of children with auditory difficulty arising from sub-cortical brain

[1] M. Monroe, *Children Who Cannot Read* (Univ. Chicago Press: 1932).

damage. *The auditory-somatic group* have very severe speech defects or no intelligible speech at all: they can learn to read by using visual and motor channels. She suggests that they should not be 'talked at' or pressed to try to listen to or simulate speech, though they might respond to lip-reading. The degree of auditory loss in these children may vary from time to time, but hearing aids may be of no use because the deafness is perceptual or central and not due to failure in the ear itself.

The auditory-autonomic group can hear but are unable to interpret what they hear; they can, however, reproduce sounds and sound patterns in a rather mechanical, stereotyped way. They have difficulty in 'finding' words and in concept building which involves the manipulation of words and grammatical structures. Their reactions to speech are often variable—sometimes they appear to understand and give correct responses to questions but at other times they react like a profoundly deaf child. Because of this variation they may be wrongly diagnosed and misunderstood. Again they usually learn to read when their visual and kinaesthetic abilities are used. Meaning from speech and reading can be facilitated by the frequent use of mime and gesture, and by relating speech and mime to visual impressions using objects, pictures and movement. Much use should be made of writing, e.g. it may be found that questions which cannot be answered satisfactorily when posed orally are often correctly answered when set and answered in writing. Again they can often answer questions when asked to use mime, e.g. 'Show me how you use this' is easier for them than 'Tell me what this is.'

Appendix I

A suggested Diagnostic Assessment Record Sheet as used in St. Francis Residential School

City of Birmingham Education Committee
St. Francis Residential School
King's Heath, Birmingham, 14

INITIAL DIAGNOSTIC ASSESSMENT

NAME .... DATE OF BIRTH.......................
DATE OF ADMISSION .... AGE ON ADMISSION ....

I. CASE HISTORY SUMMARY

2. INTELLIGENCE

W.I.S.C. DATE OF TEST.......................

Verbal tests	*Scaled score*	*Performance tests*	*Scaled score*
Information	....	Picture Completion	....
Comprehension	....	Picture Arrangement	....
Arithmetic	....	Block Design	....
Similarities	....	Object Assembly	....
Vocabulary	....	Coding	....
(Digit Span)	....	(Mazes)	....

Verbal I.Q. ....
Performance I.Q. ....
Full Scale I.Q. ....

Previous test results
Test I.Q. Date

Remarks:

....

RAVEN PROGRESSIVE MATRICES DATE OF TEST...................
I.Q.......................................
Percentile Rank ....
Classification ....

3. EDUCATIONAL STATUS

NEALE ANALYSIS OF READING ABILITY DATE OF TEST ....

Accuracy Age ....
Comprehension Age ....
Speed Age ....
Qualitative Assessment:

....

NUMBER ATTAINMENT DATE OF TEST ....

---

4. LANGUAGE DEVELOPMENT

ILLINOIS TEST OF PSYCHOLINGUISTIC ABILITIES

DATE OF TEST..

	REPRESENTATIONAL LEVEL						AUTOMATIC–SEQUENTIAL		
	Decoding		Association		Encoding		Automatic	Sequential	
	1	2	3	4	5	6	7	8	9
L.A.	Auditory	Visual	Auditory Vocal	Visual Motor	Vocal	Motor	Auditory Vocal	Auditory Vocal	Visual Motor
8–6									
8–0									
7–6									
7–0									
6–6									
6–0									
5–6									
5–0									
4–6									
4–0									
3–6									
3–0									

....

ENGLISH PICTURE VOCABULARY TEST

DATE OF TEST......................

Language Age..............................

Percentile Rank......................

5. PERCEPTION

SENSORY CHANNELS DATE OF TEST ....

1. Haptic-Visual ....
2. Kinaesthetic-Visual ....
3. Kinaesthetic-Haptic ....

....

ST. FRANCIS PERCEPTUAL PROGRAMME

1. Hand–eye Co-ordination........
2. Classifying Shapes ....
3. Naming Shapes ....
4. Form Perception ....
5. Visual Copying ....
6. Visual Retention ....
7. Visual Discrimination ....
8. Visual Sequencing..............
9. Visual Rhythm ....
10. Closure/Completion ....
11. Temporal Sequencing ....
12. Auditory Rhythm ....

Key

0 = Very Good 1 = Good 2 = Uncertain 3 = Poor 4 = Very Poor

....

Copying standard figures

Example of Child's Copy									

....

'DRAW A MAN'

Mental age .... years

Perceptual/Motor Assessment:

V. Good/Good/Average/Poor/V. Poor

Remarks:

....

BENDER VISUAL MOTOR-GESTALT TEST

Maturation Level

Remarks:

....

BENTON VISUAL RETENTION TEST

No. of designs correctly reproduced..................

General Intelligence Level ....

No. of errors ....

General Intelligence Level ....

....

HARRIS LATERALITY DOMINANCE TEST

Knowledge of Left and Right	Confused	Hesitant	Normal
Hand Dominance	L	M	R
Eye Dominance	L	M	R
Foot Dominance	L	M	R

---

6. PERSONALTY ASSESSMENT (Name any tests used)

---

7. NEUROLOGICAL EXAMINATION
Brain-Damaged/Possibly Brain-Damaged/Not Brain-Damaged
Remarks:

....

NEUROLOGICAL ASSESSMENT
Normal / Doubtful / Abnormal
Remarks:

---

8. ANY ADDITIONAL COMMENTS

Appendix II

Actual examples of reports based on the Initial Diagnostic Assessment which are given to class teachers in the school

EXAMPLE 1

S.H. Boy. C.A. $9\frac{3}{12}$ years Reading: Nil.
W.I.S.C. Verbal I.Q. = 62. Performance I.Q. = 44. Full I.Q. = 47.
(High Vocabulary Score.)

Strong evidence from neurological examination, case history, and perceptual tests of brain damage and neurological abnormality. His main weaknesses in perception are in visual and auditory rhythm and visual-motor activity. His drawing of a man indicates lack of awareness of body parts and body schema; laterality has not been thoroughly established.

He is already having a programme designed to assist neurological organization and to improve awareness of his own body.

He is also having perceptual training. Every opportunity should be taken to supplement this work in the classroom situation, e.g. by talking to him, getting him to model in plasticine and to explore things haptically.

There are signs of perseveration.

He is hyperactive and efforts should be made to slow him down, e.g. by giving quiet, slow instructions and insisting on slow, clearly enunciated answers and conversation, and slower, more precise movements.

He is not ready for reading, but already improvements are obvious, e.g. he can now match words as a visual discrimination exercise. I am hopeful that this boy will make eventual progress when we have concentrated on his neurology and perception.

(Jan. 67. Now made successful start to reading.)

EXAMPLE 2

W.P. Boy. C.A. $11\frac{9}{12}$ years. Reading: Nil.
W.I.S.C. Verbal I.Q. = 75. Performance I.Q. = 74. Full I.Q. = 72.

Neurological examination reveals that he is possibly brain-damaged and neurologically abnormal. Case history information gives no evidence but there is possible support from results on the St. Francis Perceptual Programme. His particular difficulties appear to be concerned with visual-motor activity. However, these difficulties do not appear to be so great that he will be unable to make a satisfactory start to reading almost immediately (there may be motivational problems at first).

Contrary to our usual practice, it is suggested that because he has good auditory rhythm and memory he should be taught reading by a phonic method from the beginning. I would suggest therefore that he might start on the Royal Road Reading Scheme (or I.T.A.—there may be difficulties in transferring to traditional orthography). He would quickly benefit from intensive exercises in visual discrimination and visual sequencing. These exercises should be backed by much use of language because his I.T.P.A. profile and his W.I.S.C. result show that he can make good use of language, e.g. his highest scores on I.T.P.A. are vocal encoding and automatic language and his highest W.I.S.C. Scaled Score is 10 on Comprehension.

Because of slight neurological abnormality and some uncertainty in laterality it has been arranged for him to join the new neurological group when it is formed. He should respond quickly and return to normal classroom programme in a few weeks.

EXAMPLE 3

B.C. Boy. C.A. $14\frac{8}{12}$ years. Reading: 4·2 (Burt). 5·1 (Schonell)
W.I.S.C. Verbal I.Q. = 67. Performance I.Q. = 72. Full I.Q. = 67

No evidence of brain injury or neurological abnormality; has deformity of chest but this is no handicap to him.

He is completely left-sided, but I would like the teacher to let me know if there is any real problem in left-hand/eye co-ordination.

There are no perceptual problems on our programme—standard figures are well drawn; I.T.P.A. scores indicate no specific weaknesses.

This boy's problems appear to be mainly motivational; he ought to make rapid progress here. He is withdrawn and fearful of more failure so feelings of success must be maintained. The teacher should do everything possible to bring him out of his shell and encourage him to talk and to take responsibility.

N.B. There may be reversal tendencies—please concentrate on left–right scanning of words.

(Jan. 67. Excellent start to reading.)

EXAMPLE 4

D.B. Girl. C.A. $8\frac{10}{12}$ years. Reading: Nil.
W.I.S.C. Verbal I.Q. = 76. Performance I.Q. = too low to score.
Full I.Q. = 54.

Neurological examination, results on all perceptual tests, and case history information support a diagnosis of brain injury.

Her particular difficulties are in the visuo-motor and visuo-spatial areas of perception. Movements generally are poor and crawling and creeping patterns have not been established. However, she is strongly right-sided—right-handed, right-footed, right-eyed.

Haptic-visual integration is very good, but kinaesthetic-visual, kinaesthetic-haptic, and hand–eye co-ordination are very poor. Auditory rhythm is good (it has improved dramatically after only a short period of training) and she uses language quite well. Her I.T.P.A. profile highlights her visuo-motor weaknesses and her auditory-vocal relative strengths. She is, of course, unable to draw a human figure, Bender drawings and the Standard Figures.

D.B. has very acute learning problems but she is a sweet, co-operative girl and can make use of language (she did quite well on the temporal sequencing exercises for instance). She is receiving treatment for neurological organization and is having perceptual training.

I am delighted with the progress she has made so far. There have been encouraging improvements in her movements and her visual-motor perceptual difficulties appear to be yielding to training. Her learning problems were so great that teaching her to read seemed an impossible task. There are now hopeful signs that she will make progress (she now begins to recognize words and is keen to read).

(Jan. 67. Excellent reading progress now.)

Appendix III

Equipment suitable for supplementing the perceptual training programme.

Apparatus	*Publisher*
1 **Classification of shapes**	
Inset Board	Arnolds
Posting Cabinet	Arnolds
Shapes and Colours	Arnolds
Geometric Dominoes	Galts
Shape Sorting (Train, Ship, etc.)	Arnolds
Finding Groups	Galts
Geometric Shape Spotting	Galts
Name and Shape (Game for Two)	Galts
2 **Using shapes**	
Poleidoblocs	E.S.A.
Mosaic Shapes	E.S.A.
Jigsaws	Galts
Interlocking pieces	E.S.A.
Tile Craft	Galts
Lego Sets	Galts
Tap Tap	E.S.A.
Hammer Pictures	E.S.A.
3 **Hand-eye co-ordination**	
Ring Board	
Balls	
Skittles	
Bead Threading	
Nuts and Bolts	
Simple Woodwork	
Mazes	
Fishing Game	

Apparatus	*Publisher*
4 **Form perception**	
Colour and Shape Discrimination	E.S.A.
Boats	
Flowers, etc.	
Boy and Girl Jigsaw	Galts
Peg Board	Galts
Top and Tails	E.S.A.
5 **Visual discrimination**	
Farm Animal Sets	E.S.A.
Kitchen, Living Room, Bedroom	E.S.A.
Picture Lotto	E.S.A.
Picture Dominoes	E.S.A.
Shape Dominoes	E.S.A.
Which go together? Where do they live? What do they eat? Who uses what?	Arnolds
Same and not the same	E.S.A.
Match the picture	E.S.A.
Snappy Snap	Arnolds
Pairs	E.S.A.
Spot the Set	Galts
Fit a Space	E.S.A.
6 **Temporal sequencing**	
Look and find the story	E.S.A.
7 **Auditory rhythm**	
Morse Code Signalling Set	
Tambourine. Maracas, etc.	

Addresses of Publishers

E.S.A. Ltd.,
Pinnacles,
Harlow, Essex.

James Galt & Co. Ltd.,
Brookfield Road,
Cheadle, Cheshire.

E. J. Arnold & Son Ltd.,
Butterley Street,
Leeds, 10.

Suggested additional reading

FROSTIG, M., LEFEVER, W., and WHITTLESEY, J. R. B., *Marianne Frostig Developmental Test of Visual Perception*, Consulting Psychologists Press, Palo Alto, California, 1964.

HUNT, J. MC., *Intelligence and Experience*, The Ronald Press Co., New York, 1961.

MONEY, JOHN (ed.), *Reading Disability. Progress and Research. Needs in Dyslexia*, The Johns Hopkins Press, Baltimore, 1962.

RAPAPORT, D., *Diagnostic Psychological Testing*, vol. I, The Year Book Publishers, Chicago, 1946.

SIEGEL, E., *Helping the Brain-Injured Child*, Association for Brain-injured Children, New York, 1962.

STRAUSS, A. A., and LEHTINEN, L. E., *Psychopathology and Education of the Brain-injured Child*, Grune & Stratton, New York, 1947.

WALTER, W. GRAY, *The Living Brain*, W. W. Norton, New York, 1953.

MORRIS, JOYCE M., *Standards and Progress in Reading*, Nat. Found. for Educ. Res., 1967.

Index

Page numbers in bold type indicate where topic is chiefly discussed